LEARNING RESOURCES CTR/NEW ENGLAND TECH.
GEN   E169.02.H353
Hannau, Hans   The U.S.A. book /

3 0147 0000 5539 5

E169.02.H353

Hanna

W9-CZB-654

CANADA

DAKOTA

MINNESOTA

Lake Superior

MAINE

Augusta

St. Paul

WISCONSIN

Lake Huron

Montpelier

Portland

Pierre

Minneapolis

Madison

MICHIGAN

Lansing

Lake Ontario

NEW YORK

VERMONT

NEW HAMPSHIRE

Concord

Sioux Falls

IOWA

Milwaukee

Detroit

Lake Erie

Buffalo

Albany

Boston

MASSACHUSETTS

Omaha

Des Moines

Chicago

South Bend

Cleveland

PENNSYLVANIA

Pittsburgh

Hartford

Providence

CONNECTICUT

oln

ILLINOIS

INDIANA

OHIO

Columbus

Harrisburg

New York

NEW JERSEY

Missouri River

Peoria

Indianapolis

Trenton

Atlantic City

DELAWARE

Kansas City

Springfield

Charleston

Philadelphia

Dover

Topeka

St. Louis

Louisville

WEST VIRGINIA

Washington

Baltimore

MARYLAND

Wichita

Jefferson City

Frankfort

Richmond

ATLANTIC OCEAN

MISSOURI

KENTUCKY

VIRGINIA

Norfolk

Tulsa

ARKANSAS

Nashville

Knoxville

NORTH CAROLINA

Raleigh

Oklahoma City

Mississippi River

TENNESSEE

Charlotte

OKLAHOMA

Little Rock

Atlanta

Columbia

SOUTH CAROLINA

Dallas

MISSISSIPPI

Birmingham

Columbus

Savannah

Ft. Worth

LOUISIANA

ALABAMA

Charleston

Austin

Jackson

Montgomery

GEORGIA

Baton Rouge

Mobile

Tallahassee

Jacksonville

Houston

New Orleans

Orlando

St. John

Tampa

FLORIDA

St. Thomas

Miami

San Juan

PUERTO RICO

VIRGIN ISLANDS

Ponce

Key West

St. Croix

GULF OF MEXICO

THE U·S·A· BOOK

Hans W. Hannau

THE U.S.A. BOOK

With **150** color photographs

DOUBLEDAY & COMPANY INC.
GARDEN CITY, NEW YORK

487-23

*This book about the Land we love is dedicated
to my grandchildren Lauri and Kim,
Michael, Bob, John and Linda.*

Hans Hannau

COVER DESIGN BY *DON PLATT*
MAPS BY *HEDY EIBUSCHUTZ*

ISBN: 0.385 — 12396 — 5
*ALL RIGHTS RESERVED. NO PART OF THIS WORK MAY BE REPRODUCED IN ANY FORM OR BY ANY MEANS
WITHOUT WRITTEN PERMISSION OF THE PUBLISHER.*
COMPOSED IN U.S.A.
PRINTED IN SPAIN.
D.L.B.-42,782-76

CONTENTS

THE LAND AND
THE PEOPLE

THE LAND

The United States of America, the world's fourth largest country in area, occupies the broad temperate-zone band of the continent of North America. Stretching some 3000 miles from the Atlantic Ocean in the east to the Pacific Ocean in the west and extending some 1500 miles from Canada in the north to Mexico in the south are 48 of the country's 50 states, the area known as the conterminous United States. Alaska, the 49th state, occupies the northwestern corner of North America and is thus part of the continental United States. Hawaii, the 50th state, lies 2000 miles off the west coast, in the Pacific Ocean. The United States also includes island territories in the Caribbean, such as the Commonwealth of Puerto Rico and the U.S. Virgin Islands, and island territories in the Pacific, such as American Samoa and Guam.

In ages past the North American land mass was inundated by oceans and carved by glaciers. The continent's oldest stone formations, those of the Laurentian Shield, date from the Archeozoic era of 2 billion years ago. Rocks of volcanic origin, they stretch from the Great Lakes to New England. The next oldest formations, the sedimentary rocks of the Proterozoic era of some 1.8 billion years ago, include the Huronian rocks, great iron-bearing strata in the vicinity of Lake Superior.

In the Paleozoic era, some 500 million years ago, the territory that now forms the United States was composed of five great land masses bordering on an inland sea whose sediment constitutes a vast repository of evolving life. During that era natural gas, petroleum, lead, marble, zinc, and a host of other minerals were deposited in the sands, and at that time the greatest coal beds known to man, those of the eastern United States, were formed.

Dinosaurs inhabited the swamps that existed along the Atlantic coast during the Mesozoic era that began 200 million years ago. It was the era in which the earth's crust along the Pacific coast began to buckle and the highlands of the western United States were lifted up. The sea returned and filled the area between the Appalachians of the east and the newly-formed mountains of the west.

The North American continent swarmed with animal life in the glacial Pleistocene epoch, which began perhaps a million or more years ago. Mastodons, mammoths, elephants, now-extinct breeds of horses, saber-toothed tigers, cave bears, tapirs, bison, and musk oxen roamed the land. But as great sheets of ice spread, cutting huge gouges in the earth, the animals were driven southward. Eventually more than half of North America lay buried beneath layers of ice. Gradually the ice sheets began to retreat, and as they melted they deposited blankets of sediment. That was the time when man gained the ascendancy. Somewhere, perhaps in Central Asia, Homo sapiens stood erect and began to walk over the new grasslands. And in the course of time he walked all the way to North America.

The face of the United States today is marked by three major north-south mountain systems — the Appalachians, in the east; the Rockies; and the Sierra-Cascade, in the far west. The mountains long slowed the peopling and development of the United States. But intrepid pioneers cut trails from the Atlantic to the Pacific; railroad tracks, telegraph lines, and highways appeared; and eventually air routes and radio communications tied together the continental nation to form a united country.

The Appalachian system, a band of old mountains, ridges, clay hills, and river valleys, extends from Canada in the north to Alabama in the south. The White Mountains of New Hampshire, Vermont's Green Mountains, the Blue Ridge Mountains of Virginia and North Carolina, and the Smokies of Tennessee are all part of the Appalachian system, as are the Adirondacks of New York and the Alleghenies that stretch from Pennsylvania to West Virginia. Highest of the Appalachian peaks, which average about 4000 feet in height, are Mt. Washington in New Hampshire, with an elevation of 6288 feet, and Mt. Mitchell in North Carolina, which rises to a height of 6684 feet. The region has rich mineral deposits and forests, and there are fertile soils. East of the Appalachians, between the highlands and the Atlantic Ocean, is a 100 to 200 mile wide coastal plain — narrow, rocky, and hilly in the north; wider, flatter, and more fertile in the south.

West of the Appalachians stretches a vast plain, 1500 miles across at its widest. It extends the length of the continent, from the Arctic in the north to the Gulf of Mexico in the south. Cutting through this plain is the mighty Mississippi River, which flows for more than 3500 miles from its beginning in northern Minnesota to the Gulf of Mexico. The Mississippi is fed from the east by the Ohio River, which itself waters a fertile valley. The principal tributary of the west is the Missouri River. The vast drainage basin of the Mississippi system involves territory of more than 30 states.

West of the Mississippi River the plains rise gradually to an elevation of 6000 feet at the edge of the Rockies. In this western area are the huge, somewhat arid plains of Texas, underlain by rich petroleum deposits, and the mesas of Oklahoma, which give a sense of flow to the land. Also part of this huge plains area are the rich farmlands of Kansas and Nebraska. Buffalo once roamed the broad grasslands, and the soil is generally good. But vast areas have suffered drought, and in the 1930's part of the western plains became a huge Dust Bowl.

The Rockies may be said to mark the beginning of the West. These steep-sloped, snow-capped mountains form part of a great continental upland, the Cordilleras of North America, which extend from Alaska to Central America. Included in the Rocky Mountain system are the Teton Range, the Laramie Mountains, and others. The peaks of the Rockies rise to 14,000 feet, and the highest, Mt. Elbert in Colorado, soars 14,433 feet.

To the south and west the Rockies fall off to high, dry plateaus broken by still other small mountain ranges. Death Valley in California, the Great Salt Lake of Utah, and Arizona's Grand Canyon of the Colorado River are among the natural features of

11

this spectacular region.

Beyond the high inland basin area lie the Sierra Nevada and Cascade ranges, a mountain barrier that extends from Canada to southern California. The Sierra-Cascade system includes some of the highest mountains of North America south of Alaska — Mt. Rainier in Washington, 14,410 feet high; and Mt. Whitney in California, 14,494 feet in elevation.

Between the Sierra-Cascade peaks and the Pacific are long, fertile valleys, important producers of fruits and vegetables for the entire United States. The Pacific coast itself is a rocky shoreline broken by stretches of fine beaches and great bays offering deep-water anchorages.

The wind patterns of the United States are responsible for one of the country's most attractive features, its frequent changes of weather. The prevailing winds move across the wide country from west to east, and the varied weather they bring makes everything seem to change from day to day. In the north, cyclones and blizzards alternate with sunny, blue skies; in the south, heavy autumnal rains are broken by clear days when all appears green and gold.

Extremes of temperature are an everyday way of life in many parts of the United States. The lowest temperature recorded was –66°F on a February day in Yellowstone National Park, and the highest, 134°F, was recorded one July in Death Valley. Winters in New England, the Great Plains, and the entire northern tier of states, as well as in the Rockies, tend to be extremely cold, whereas frost is moderate in the south, except in mountain areas, and the Gulf Coast and southern Florida are free of frost. The Pacific coast registers little variation in temperature. Summers in the northeast and northwest are generally pleasant, but summer temperatures in the interior plains are high. Warm, wet air moves over the Gulf states in summer and into fall.

The trees and flowers, birds and animals of the United States are as varied as the weather. In the coldest zones, which are found at the highest elevations of the White Mountains in New England and of the Rockies and Sierra-Cascade in the West, as well as in Alaska, there are few plants and animals. Spruce, balsam, aspen, pine, and birch grow in the Hudsonian and Canadian temperature zones, the home, in the western mountains, of the mountain goat and the mountain sheep. The Canadian zone is warmer in the east, where it includes much of New England, the Adirondacks and Catskills, and the higher elevations of the Appalachians southward into Tennessee, than along the lower slopes of the western ranges. Fir and hemlock and other deciduous trees shelter lynx, moose, caribou, and many smaller animals such as beaver.

The transitional zone of the Alleghenies in the east is a world of magnificent deciduous forests — walnut, oak, hickory, beech, birch, sugar maple, elm and pine. The transitional zone of the Pacific region has stands of giant sequoia, huge Douglas fir, Sitka spruce, and Pacific cedar. In the transitional zone of the arid western areas are sagebrush and some pine.

The lower forest zone in the eastern half of the country includes the great woodlands of the Carolinas, where the tulip tree, sycamore, pine, magnolia, oak, bald cypress, and tupelo are found. In the west, this zone is the home of mesquite, cactus, creosote bushes, and yucca. The tropical belt includes southern Florida, with its palm trees and mangrove, and Hawaii, with its full range of lush vegetation.

THE PEOPLE

The history of man in what is now the United States is a story that still intrigues the archaeologist and the anthropologist, the linguist and the historian, the zoologist and the geologist. There is no indication that any type of man originated in North America, for the oldest remains that have been found are those of Homo sapiens, modern man.

Among the earliest evidences of human habitation are tools of the Sandia culture of the Southwest and of hunters in Texas, Nevada, and Florida, which are believed to be some 20,000 to 30,000 years old. Other archaeological finds may place man in North America earlier. But the determination of dates is extremely difficult, and even modern techniques such as radioactive carbon procedures provide but broad approximations.

Where those early people came from is also unknown. Many scholars believe that man migrated to the New World from the Old over a land bridge that once connected North America and Asia at present-day Bering Strait. Others hold that there were oceanic migrations. Both may well be right, for there developed very different societies, and many different New World language groups have been recognized. The Aztecs of Mexico, with their highly accurate calendar and written language; the Pueblo peoples of the Southwest; and the copper-working people of Wisconsin reflect the wide diversity of early man in North America.

The number of people living in what is now the United States and Canada when the Spanish first arrived in the 1500s has been estimated by various scholars at from 1 to 2 million. Unlike their far more numerous neighbors to the south in Mexico and Central America and in South America, they had not developed civilizations with monumental buildings and writing systems. The "Indians," as they came to be called, who lived in North America north of Mexico were predominantly hunters and fishers and farmers.

The first contacts between Europeans and American Indians in this land came when the Spanish explorers extended their search for treasure beyond the Caribbean and Mexico. In the early 1500s, Juan Ponce de León was driven away from Florida by Calusa Indians; later, in the 1530s, Hernando de Soto landed on the west coast of Florida and made his way northward and westward against the opposition of the

Indians. Failure to find treasure, and the hostility of the Indians, led the Spanish to halt their explorations of the present-day United States for a time, and it was not until 1565 that they founded their first permanent settlement, St. Augustine, Florida.

France, too, became interested in the New World, and between 1533 and 1541 Jacques Cartier made three voyages up the St. Lawrence River. He too failed to find riches comparable to those found in Mexico and South America, and the first permanent French settlements in what is now Canada were not made for another 60 years.

In the reign of Queen Elizabeth I, England became a serious contender in the contest for North American colonies. The first English colony, founded by Sir Walter Raleigh in Virginia, foundered; but the settlement made at Jamestown in 1607 survived. The English, too, failed to find the gold they sought, but the Indians of the Powhattan Confederacy they met taught them to grow tobacco, which proved to be a source of riches. The Indians also showed them how to grow potatoes, tomatoes, corn, and sea-island cotton, a long-staple variety superior to other types. Despite the generosity of the Indians, the English settlers' drive for land soon led to conflict and the English began a policy of driving the Indians from the James River region.

To the north, in the Delaware River area and at the mouth of the Hudson, the Dutch established trading posts. They sought furs from the Indians, not land, and relations between the Europeans and the Indians were peaceful for a time. But peaceful relations in what became New York soon became bloody as the Dutch settlement grew, and the Indians were forced from the land.

Captain John Smith held together the first successful English colony, which settled at the head of the James River in Virginia in 1607. It was backed financially by a company of London merchants, the Virginia Company, for the purpose of trade "with friends and natural kinsmen." During the starving time of Jamestown's first years one man killed his wife and salted her, Captain Smith reported. The man was executed.

Captain Smith explored, wrote, propagandized in England, and the colony grew stronger. Immigrants were tempted by payment of their passage to Virginia and by grants of fifty acres of land. English common law was introduced into the colony at the first colonial legislature in 1619. In 1624 Virginia became a Royal Colony, as a result of financial shennanigans of the Virginia Company.

16

THE PEOPLE

A European colony in New England was established in 1620, at Plymouth, by the Pilgrims. Their vessel, the *Mayflower*, had set out for Virginia, but after a stormy voyage they landed on Cape Cod. The new colonists were met by friendly Indians who taught them how to plant corn, showed them where to fish, and helped them to establish themselves in their new homeland. But within two decades the English settlers and the Indians were at war, and again the Indians were forced to leave their lands.

This became the story of the European settlement of the United States: Indians retreating before advancing English colonists, moving westward, and eventually being decimated. Today, even after decades of "peace," the Indian population of the United States is perhaps some 750,000, considerably less than at the time European colonization began some three centuries ago.

In the 1600s and early 1700s, the American Indian captured the imagination of Europeans. While the battles to exterminate them were going on in North America, the myth of the Noble Savage was enchanting European romantics. Today white Americans, many of whom came to share the romantic view of the country's earliest inhabitants, have begun to adopt a more realistic attitude. And the American Indian is expressing his needs and desires, and he is beginning to be heard.

The early settlers of the United States were a varied lot, spurred to leave the Old World for many reasons. Some, such as the first settlers of Virginia, came in search of land and opportunity. Others, such as the first New England colonists, sought a land where they could worship as they thought right. Still others sought respite from the wars that plagued Europe in the 1600s and 1700s. All, however, sought something better than they had known.

The first "involuntary" immigrants were Africans. Blacks had participated in the Spanish explorations of the Americas in the 1500s, but the first to be brought to the North American English colonies arrived in Virginia in 1619 on a Dutch ship. They were indentured servants, not slaves, but within little more than a half century colonial Virginia passed the first regulations distinguishing between blacks and whites on the basis of color, and black indentured servants became black slaves. As the plantation economy of the South developed, the need for field labor grew and more and more people of African origin were brought to the country as slaves. Although the importation of slaves officially ended in 1808, the number of black slaves continued to increase, and by the mid-1800s may have reached a total of more than 4 million.

The abolition of slavery as a result of the Civil War did not bring to black Americans the opportunities for full participation in the nation's cultural, economic, or political life, however. Restrictive legislation was adopted in many areas of the country, and black and white Americans were separated — by law in some parts of the nation; by custom in other sections. By the 1960s, though, when the black population represented at least 10 percent of the country's total, black Americans had begun to act and to speak with new vigor. They successfully challenged laws they felt discriminatory, and a new generation of black leaders emerged as spokesmen. Although often divided on both goals and means, Americans of African ancestry are increasingly taking their places in the mainstream of national life.

The 1800s were years of tremendous European immigration. The early decades saw a continuation of established patterns, with the overwhelming majority coming from northern Europe, especially the British Isles. Famine in Ireland in the 1840s led thousands of Irish to the United States, where they tended to settle in the urban centers along the eastern seaboard. At about the same time, economic and political difficulties in Central Europe led many Germans to emigrate to the United States.

Immigration slowed during the Civil War, but revived immediately after during a period of economic expansion. Asians joined Europeans in seeking work in the New World, and many thousands of Chinese entered California after the discovery of gold in 1849. Japanese immigrants soon joined them, but the folk-myth of the "Yellow Peril" led to legislation and other forms of national action to limit Asian immigration.

Beginning in the 1870s the pattern of immigration from Europe began to change. Increasing numbers of people from southern and eastern Europe began to arrive in the United States. Italians and Slavs and East European Jews arrived in the cities of the Northeast in large numbers, and they carried with them distinctive life-styles that contrasted with those of the predominantly English-speaking majority.

In 1921 the U.S. Congress passed legislation establishing national origin quotas for those seeking to come to the United States. The quotas were based on the census of 1910 and favored immigrants from northern Europe. An annual limit was also placed on the number of people who could enter the United States. A new law in 1924 further restricted immigration and went back to the census of 1890 as the basis for establishing national origin quotas, further restricting immigration from southern and eastern Europe. Asian immigration was virtually eliminated. Attitudes in the United States gradually changed, however, in part under the impact of World War II, and in 1965 the Congress abolished the national origin quota system.

Despite the limitations imposed on immigration, the United States remained open to immigrants on an emergency basis. Immediately after World War II, hundreds of thousands of displaced persons found new homes in the United States, and in 1956 many thousands of Hungarians were admitted after an unsuccessful attempt to secure greater freedom in their land. And after Fidel Castro came to power in Cuba in 1959, many, many thousands of refugees from that country were allowed to take up residence in the United States.

Accompanying the movement of millions of people from other lands to the United States has been a constant internal movement of people westward. The men who blazed the pioneer trails to the West have been enshrined in myth, but they existed. Daniel Boone led the way through the Appalachians, establishing the Wilderness Road over the Cumberland Gap. Davy Crockett led the way west from Tennessee all the way to Texas, where he died at the siege of the Alamo in 1836. Kit Carson guided explorer John Frémont on his expedition to the West in the 1840s. Other names come to mind, including Meriwether Lewis and William Clark, sent by President Thomas Jefferson to explore the vast territory acquired by the Louisiana Purchase in 1803, and Zebulon Pike, now best remembered for the Colorado peak that bears his name.

Many men, women, and children moved west in covered wagons in the 1840s determined to reach the fabled Oregon. Others moved westward with the discovery of gold in California. Reasons other than new and better farmland and gold fever drew people to the American West. In the 1840s the Mormons, members of the Church of Jesus Christ of Latter-day Saints, were forced by persecution to leave the East, where their religion had been founded. They eventually reached the area that is now the state of Utah, and there they built a prosperous community.

Another great trek to California came in the 1880s, when the Santa Fe Railroad reached southern California. In the 1930s drought struck large areas of the Southwest, and many families left their farms in what had become a Dust Bowl for the green lands of southern California, where they became the "Okies," immortalized by John Steinbeck in his novel *The Grapes of Wrath.* The discovery of rich oil deposits and the development of a vast industrial complex centering around the aircraft industry during and after World War II drew still more people to California. And by 1970 the Golden State, as California came to be called, was the most populous in the nation.

The great drive westward did not stop at California. Intrepid souls pushed on across the Pacific to Hawaii and northward to Alaska, which was acquired by the United States from Russia in the 1860s. Gold drew many to Alaska in the 1890s, and in the depression years of the 1930s the federal government aided settlers in building new homes in the fertile Matanuska Valley. A newer magnet appeared in the 1960s and 1970s with the discovery of oil and the beginnings of its exploitation. And perhaps today Alaska is the last frontier for the seemingly perpetually westward-bound American.

THE NATION

THE NATION

The last of the 13 English North American colonies, Georgia, was chartered in 1733, and within two decades Benjamin Franklin offered a plan of union for the colonies. Although the plan was rejected by both the colonial legislatures and the English government, it indicated clearly the existence of a sense of identity among the Americans.

In 1763 France ceded Canada and the Mississippi Valley with the lands east of the river (except New Orleans) to England, and Spain ceded Florida to England. But the costs of the imperial struggles of Europe were reflected in British colonial policies that provoked opposition in North America. In 1764 a Committee of Correspondence was formed in Boston to maintain contacts with the other 12 colonies in the face of new taxation and restrictions on the trade of the colonies. And in 1765 representatives of the 13 colonies met in New York and adopted a declaration of rights and grievances to be presented to London.

Tailors, printers and seamen began to form unions and to strike for better pay and working conditions after 1768.

In Boston the riotous and rebellious Massachusetts citizenry in 1770 clashed with English troops and the Boston Massacre resulted. The first organized resistance against the British rulers in the colonies was made by the Regulators of western North Carolina, who rebelled in 1771 against the British Governor William Tryon's way of ruling. In 1772 Rhode Islanders attacked a customs schooner.

It was, however, an act that allowed the British East India Company to sell a big surplus of duty-free tea to the colonists that really teed off the rebellious American merchants. They were being undersold, because they were stocked with tea on which they had paid duty. So, disguised as Mohawk Indians, they staged the Boston Tea Party on December 13, 1773, climbing aboard the tea ship *Dartmouth* and dumping into the Boston harbor the contents of 342 chests of tea. The English government closed the port of Boston.

Colonial reaction was expressed in the calling of the first Continental Congress at Philadelphia in 1774. All but Georgia were represented at the session, where the colonials declared that "Americans cannot submit." Tensions increased, and in 1775 Massachusetts was the scene of a major clash between English troops and Americans.

A second Continental Congress met at Philadelphia that year and named George Washington commander in chief of the colonials, who then numbered some 2.6 million. The following year the break with England was made complete with the issuance of the Declaration of Independence, drafted by Thomas Jefferson.

England attempted to put down the rising by force of arms, but the American colonials, aided by France and Spain, England's imperial rivals, held their own. By 1781 the Articles of Confederation had been drafted and approved by all 13 colonies, and in 1782 the English surrendered at Yorktown, leaving the Americans to form their new nation as they saw fit.

Not all of the inhabitants of the 13 colonies supported the struggle for independence, and many loyalists fled to England, Canada, and other parts of the empire. By 1784, when the Congress ratified the Treaty of Paris officially ending the Revolutionary War, the population of the young country was no more than 2.5 million, less than the total recorded a decade before. The exodus of those loyal to the British helped change the social structure of the new land, as well as helping to reduce its population. Among those who chose to leave were many men of wealth, including many large landowners, and the dominant group left was composed largely of those of moderate wealth and with medium sized holdings.

The fledgling nation was described in 1782 by a Frenchman, J. Hector St. John (Crèvecoeur), who had settled on a farm in New York after traveling in the colonies. In his *Letters from an American Farmer* he wrote: "Here individuals of all nations are melted into a new race of men, whose labors and posterity will one day cause great change in the world."

THE NATION

The New Government

The government of the new nation, operating under the Articles of Confederation, chose New York City as a temporary capital until a federal district could be established.

The Articles of Confederation left the Congress with little power, and the states conducted their economic affairs as they saw fit. But in 1787 a Constitutional Convention was convened in Philadelphia with all of the states but Rhode Island eventually represented. Although originally called to revise the Articles of Confederation, the meeting drafted a new document, the Constitution of the United States.

The proposed constitution was the subject of heated debate. Many, such as Patrick Henry, felt that the stronger federal government it would establish would destroy the governments of the states. Others, the Federalists, argued for acceptance. Led by Alexander Hamilton, James Madison, and John Jay, they voiced the view that a stronger central government was needed if the new country was to survive.

Within the year, Delaware, Pennsylvania, and New Jersey had ratified the Constitution, and other states followed. But a number of states insisted that the Constitution be amended to guarantee the liberties for which they had fought, and ten amendments, the Bill of Rights, were adopted by the first Congress and approved by the states. George Washington was chosen the first president of the United States under the Constitution, and on April 30, 1789 he was inaugurated in New York City.

The new country began to grow almost immediately. In 1791 Vermont was admitted to the Union as the 14th state, and in 1792 Kentucky, originally a part of Virginia, became the 15th state. National political parties were also formed. Hamilton led the Federalists and Jefferson became the leader of the Republicans, later known as the Democratic-Republicans. Economic developments also came quickly. The foundations of the textile industry were laid in Rhode Island in 1790 when the first water-powered spinning machine was put into operation, and in 1793 Eli Whitney invented the cotton gin, which greatly speeded the processing of cotton and spurred the use of slave labor in the South.

In 1792 a Boston mariner Robert Gray, reached the Columbia River, thus giving the United States a claim to the vast Pacific Northwest, and in 1803, under the administration of Thomas Jefferson, the United States purchased the huge Louisiana territory of France, doubling the area of the United States. President Jefferson sent Meriwether Lewis and William Clark to explore the lands west of the Mississippi, and in 1806, on their return to St. Louis, their starting point, they had proved that overland travel to the West was possible.

In 1808 the Congress prohibited the importation of black slaves and made it illegal for U.S. citizens to participate in the slave trade. But blacks continued to be brought into the United States illegally, and between 1808 and 1860 it has been estimated that some quarter of a million were brought here. Slavery had been made illegal in Pennsylvania, Connecticut, Rhode Island, New York, New Jersey, and Massachusetts in the 1780s, and the overwhelming majority of the country's more than 1 million slaves were held in the states of the South.

In 1812 the United States again went to war with England. The immediate cause of the struggle was British interference with U.S. shipping during England's conflict with Napoleonic France. But the struggle also involved a drive for territorial expansion and an extension of areas of white settlement in Indian lands. The war was not popular in all parts of the country, however, and Connecticut and Massachusetts, for example, refused to supply militia. A disastrous campaign aimed at taking Canada was balanced by naval victories, and the *Constitution* won its nickname of Old Ironsides. The land struggle involved intensified fighting with the Indians of the Northwest, as well as with British forces, and British troops burned part of the new capital of Washington.

Gradually U.S. forces won back the territory that had been lost, and in 1814 peace negotiations began. The Treaty of Ghent, signed in December 1814, officially ended the conflict, but the most famous battle of the war was fought two weeks later at New Orleans, where Andrew Jackson repulsed a major British attack.

Expansion

Territorial expansion accompanied the return to peace. Settlers pushed westward across the Appalachians in tremendous numbers. Construction was begun on the Erie Canal, extending from Buffalo, on Lake Erie, to Albany, on the Hudson River, and thus providing a water route linking the Great Lakes and the Atlantic.

In 1818 Andrew Jackson pushed into eastern Florida in a move against the Seminole Indians, with whom U.S. forces had been involved in skirmishes for two years. And in 1819 Spain ceded eastern Florida to the United States, which in turn relinquished claims to Texas.

American settlement in Texas began on a large scale in 1821, when the Spanish governor gave Moses Austin, father of Stephen, a charter allowing families from the United States to move to the territory. In 1825 the government of Mexico, by then an independent nation, legally opened Texas to settlement.

Living by themselves in a part of the country with little contact with Mexican national life, the settlers retained their U.S. identity and did not become Mexicans. In 1830 the Mexican government moved to end immigration from the United States and to exercise control over Texas affairs. The Texans refused to accept Mexican control and in 1833 voted in convention for separation.

The Mexican government sent troops against the secessionists and in 1836 laid siege to the Alamo, in San Antonio. Fewer than 200 men, including Davy Crockett and James Bowie, held the fort for two weeks against a Mexican force of some 3000. The Alamo fell on March 27, and the defenders were killed. A month later, led by Sam Houston, the Texans defeated the Mexican army in the Battle of San Jacinto and captured General Santa Anna.

Texas was proclaimed a republic, and Sam Houston was chosen its president. Houston sought annexation by the United States, but many members of Congress opposed such a move on the grounds that Texas would be a slave state and that annexation would be contrary to U.S. obligations to Mexico. The issue was revived in 1842, when Mexican troops entered Texas, and Britain and France intervened diplomatically.

In 1845 the Republic of Texas was annexed to the United States by joint resolution of the Congress, becoming the 28th state of the Union, and war with Mexico began in 1846. Two months after the outbreak of war, U.S. residents in California proclaimed the Bear Flag Republic in that Mexican territory, but Mexican control was quickly reestablished.

U.S. forces captured the capital of Mexico in 1847, and peace negotiations began soon thereafter. As a result of the war, the United States acquired a huge area that included the present-day states of California, Nevada, Utah, and most of Arizona, as well as what is now western Colorado and New Mexico.

The 1840s also saw U.S. expansion into the Pacific Northwest. Settlers had begun to move into the area over the Oregon Trail, which stretched from Independence, Missouri, to the mouth of the Columbia River on the Pacific coast. The influx of people from the United States created serious problems in U.S.-British relations, for the boundary had never been firmly set. Both nations had claims to the land between the Columbia River and the 49th parallel to the north, and expansionists in the United States made a boundary of 54°40″ ("or fight") a national slogan. The issue was peacefully resolved in 1846, however, when the United States accepted a British proposal to set the boundary at the 49th parallel.

Disunion

The first half of the 1800s was marked by increasing concern over the issue of slavery in the United States. The issue had slowed the admission of Texas and other states to the Union, and it had become a divisive force in national life. In the North, Abolitionist activity increased after 1830, and in 1831 the first issue of William Lloyd Garrison's the *Liberator* appeared in Boston. The Underground Railroad, which helped fugitive slaves escape from the South and find refuge in the North or in Canada, was established in 14 states. And an estimated 50,000 slaves did escape through the Underground Railroad between 1830 and 1860.

A dramatic slave revolt led by Nat Turner broke out in Virginia in 1831, and during the 1831-1832 session of the state legislature emancipation was almost approved. Defeat of the emancipation attempt was followed by the imposition of even stricter controls over slaves in Virginia and other states where slavery existed.

Southern spokesmen in Congress, which was receiving increasing numbers of petitions calling for the abolition of slavery, declared the issue to be a matter of states' rights and no concern of the federal government. And as anti-slavery forces in Congress had delayed the admission of Texas, so in 1849 did pro-slavery forces delay the admission of California, a free state. At that time there were 30 states, 15 free and 15 slave, and the Southerners feared the loss of the balance in the Senate, where each state had an equal number of votes.

A compromise was finally reached in 1850, and California was admitted to the Union. Its population had increased fivefold in no more than two years with the discovery of gold in 1848 at Sutter's Mill, in the Sacramento Valley. But the compromise failed to satisfy either side, and the issue of slavery remained unresolved.

National expansion continued despite the bitter dispute dividing the country, and in 1853 the United States acquired from Mexico through the Gadsen Purchase a 30,000-square-mile territory that included part of what is now Arizona and New Mexico. Immigration also continued, and between 1840 and 1850 some 1.7 million people arrived in the United States, bringing the total population to more than 23 million.

In 1854 Senator Stephen A. Douglas introduced in Congress the Kansas-Nebraska Act to organize the Kansas and Nebraska territories. They included not only present-day Kansas and Nebraska, but also parts of Colorado, Montana, South Dakota, North Dakota, and Wyoming. The act allowed each territorial government to decide for itself if it wished to allow slavery. A month later, forces opposed to the act, which they viewed as a slave-owners' plot, met at Ripon, Wisconsin, and urged the formation of a new political party to be called "Republican." Within a year the new party had spread throughout the North.

Both pro-slavery and anti-slavery groups sponsored settlements in the territories. The Kansas-Nebraska Act was passed in 1854, and within two years the Kansas Territory had two governments, one pro-slavery and one anti-slavery, or "Free-State." Kansas became a battleground — pro-slavery "Ruffians" attacked Lawrence, a Free-State town, and, in retaliation, Abolitionists led by John Brown attacked a pro-slavery settlement. Federal troops finally restored order.

Kansas and slavery had become dominant political issues by 1858, when an Illinois lawyer, Abraham Lincoln, won the Republican nomination for the Senate and challenged the incumbent, Stephen Douglas, to public debate. Douglas won the election, but Lincoln won national attention. An anti-slavery moderate, Lincoln was nominated for president by the Republicans in 1860, and Douglas won the Democratic nomination.

Douglas argued that territories should decide for themselves if they wished to have slavery, but a Southern group named its own candidate, who called for allowing slavery in the territories.

Lincoln won the election, which was decided along regional lines, and on December 20 South Carolina seceded from the Union, refusing to be governed by a president opposed to slavery and affirming the sovereignty of the states. Lincoln was inaugurated in March 1861, by which time seven states had seceded and formed the Confederate States of America. Alabama, Georgia, Louisiana, Mississippi, South Carolina, Florida, and Texas chose Jefferson Davis of Mississippi to be the first president of the Confederacy.

South Carolina forces fired on Fort Sumter on April 12, 1861, and Lincoln called for the raising of a militia to put down the "insurrection." The North supported his move, but four more states seceded and joined the Confederacy — Arkansas, North Carolina, Tennessee, and Virginia. Richmond, Virginia's capital, became the capital of the Confederacy. One-third of the officers of the army resigned to join the Confederacy, and among them was Robert E. Lee, who became commander of the southern armies.

It was a bloody war. The 11 Confederate states, predominantly agricultural and with a population of some 9 million, including more than 3 million slaves, opposed 23 Union states, including the most industrialized states of the country, with a population of 22 million.

Slavery was abolished in the District of Columbia and in the territories in 1861, and in 1863 President Lincoln's Emancipation Proclamation declared all slaves in areas in rebellion free.

The major battle of the war began on July 1, 1863. Lee led his Confederate forces northward into Pennsylvania and met a Union army at Gettysburg. On July 4 the Confederate forces began to pull back, having suffered 20,000 killed and wounded. A campaign of attrition was waged for two years as Union armies gradually cut through the South. General William Sherman led a Union army from Tennessee through Georgia, leaving Atlanta in ruins, and then cut northward through the Carolinas. General Ulysses Grant, commander of the Union armies, held Lee in a siege at Petersburg, Virginia. On April 9 Lee and Grant met at Appomattox Court House. Lee surrendered his army, and by the end of May all Confederate forces had put down their arms.

Lincoln had won reelection in 1864, but less than two months after his second inauguration he was assassinated in Washington's Ford's Theater by John Wilkes Booth, and Vice President Andrew Johnson of Tennessee became the 17th president of the United States. He put Lincoln's principles for dealing with the South in an amnesty and reconstruction proclamation in May 1865 and recognized provisional governments in the southern states. The Congress, dominated by men more radical than Lincoln or Johnson, refused to accept the governments recognized by the president, and the long, bitter era of Reconstruction began.

The war had taken more than 600,000 lives, left tens of thousands maimed, and had depleted the wealth of the nation. Of perhaps more importance for the history of the nation was the bitterness that remained after the hostilities had ended.

Continued Growth

The great migration westward, spurred by railroad construction and government land policies, continued. And with increased settlement, conflicts with the Indians also increased. The tribes of the eastern United States had been moved westward, to Oklahoma, but lands given them were taken away on the grounds that they had supported the Confederacy during the Civil War. Other conflicts came in Colorado, Wyoming, and Montana, where Cheyenne. Arapaho, and Sioux fought the swelling tide of settlers. Soon they too were removed from their lands, and they were settled in the Dakota Territory in 1868.

In the year before, 1867, the United States had purchased Alaska from Russia, but Secretary of State Seward's efforts to purchase the Virgin Islands from Denmark failed to win Congressional approval. But settlers did not flock to the cold, new territory.

Immigration had continued, and between 1860 and 1870 more than 2 million more people arrived in the country. The population had reached a total of almost 40 million, of whom close to 5 million were black. The 13th, 14th, and 15th amendments to the

Constitution had all been ratified before the end of 1870. They forbade slavery, made all persons born or naturalized in the United States citizens, and stated that the right of citizens to vote shall not be denied on the basis of race, color, or previous conditions of servitude.

The last of the former states of the Confederacy were readmitted to the Union in 1870, after all had accepted the three amendments to the Constitution. But organizations such as the Ku Klux Klan had been formed to limit the rights of blacks in many parts of the South, and in 1870-1871 Federal prosecution resulted in more than a thousand convictions of those who engaged in such activities.

Industrial and technological progress was rapid in the last decades of the 1800s. Refrigerated railroad cars were developed to ship fresh meat from the West over the continental rail system that had been opened in 1869, when the Union Pacific building westward from Nebraska met the Central Pacific pushing eastward from California.

Alexander Graham Bell developed the telephone and organized the Bell Telephone Company; and Thomas Edison patented the phonograph. Albert Michelson accurately measured the speed of light; and Thomas Edison's improved electric light bulb made electricity for home lighting use practical. George Selden patented the first "horseless carriage" powered by an internal combustion engine; and John Augustus Roebling's Brooklyn Bridge connected Brooklyn with Manhattan. Ottmar Mergenthaler patented the Linotype machine; and Lewis Waterman produced the first practical fountain pen.

By 1880 the population of the United States had passed the 50 million mark, and immigration accounted for almost 3 million of the 10 million increase in the decade. In 1890 the population was recorded at almost 63 million, and immigration in the ten years exceeded 5 million. In that year the census reported that the frontier had ceased to exist.

Industrial growth was accompanied by the development of trusts, and the concentrations of economic power resulted in increasing monopolies in U.S. business. In 1890 the government moved to regulate these huge business complexes through the Sherman Antitrust Act. Labor, too, was becoming organized, and in 1886 the American Federation of labor was formed in Columbus, Ohio, with Samuel Gompers as its first president.

The century ended with the continued territorial growth of the United States. Cuba's struggle for independence from Spain began in 1895, and the Cubans won the sympathy of the United States. In 1898 the U.S. warship *Maine*, lying in the harbor of Havana to protect U.S. interests in Cuba, blew up with the loss of more than 200 lives. War with Spain quickly followed.

U.S. troops landed in Cuba, and the U.S. Pacific fleet went into action in the Pacific, where Spain had other colonial holdings. The war was brief, ending in the same year. Cuba won its independence, and the United States won Puerto Rico and, in the Pacific, the island of Guam and the Philippines. The U.S. presence in the Pacific was further strengthened in 1898, when President William McKinley signed the annexation of Hawaii bill, and in 1899, when the United States and Germany divided Samoa between them.

A New Century

President McKinley was assassinated in 1901, and Vice President Theodore Roosevelt became president of the United States. The nation had grown to 76 million, increasing by more than a fifth in a decade, and some 40 percent of the people of the United States lived in cities and towns of more than 2500. New York, the largest city, had more than 3 million inhabitants and Chicago, the second largest, had a population of well over a million and a half. More than 3.6 million immigrants had arrived in the country since 1890, bringing the total since 1820 to more than 19 million.

The United States, with its overseas territories, had also become a world power, and it played an increasing role in world diplomacy.

The opening years of the new century saw the Wright brothers fly at Kitty Hawk, North Carolina, and the Olds Company begin the mass production of automobiles at Detroit, Michigan. Rayon became the first successfully produced synthetic fiber, and Leo Baekeland patented his plastic, Bakelite.

Theodore Roosevelt, who had won fame as one of the Rough Riders of the Spanish-American War, quickly indicated that he would be a vigorous president. He announced in his first annual message that he intended to enforce the Sherman Antitrust Act, and he won the title of "trust buster." He also intervened in a widespread strike of coal miners in Pennsylvania, insisting on arbitration in the face of mine-owner opposition. A month after becoming president, Roosevelt gave a White House luncheon for black educator Booker T. Washington.

Roosevelt also undertook an active role in international affairs. The United States won the right to build a canal across the Isthmus of Panama; Roosevelt, at the request of Venezuela, intervened diplomatically in that country's disputes with European nations; and in 1905 he mediated the Russo–Japanese War, winning the 1906 Nobel Peace Prize for his efforts.

The imagination of the nation was captured in 1909, when Robert Perry with Matthew Henson and four Eskimos reached the North Pole. But the key to the future life-style of the nation, Henry Ford's Model T auto, had gone into production the year before. Produced at a cost of $850 in 1908, by 1926 Ford was able to sell the car for only $310. A new industrial revolution had begun, the assembly line had arrived.

Woodrow Wilson, a Democrat and former president of Princeton University, was elected president of the United States in 1912. He had been opposed by William Howard Taft, Republican; Theodore Roosevelt, running as an independent; and Eugene V. Debs, Socialist. Debs received more than 900,000 votes, a reflection of increased concern with social problems in the United States.

Socialists had won election as mayor in a number of cities, and social legislation became more frequent. In 1912, for example, Massachusetts passed the first minimum wage law; New York adopted a law limiting the work week to 54 hours; and Congress passed a bill establishing the eight-hour-day for federal employees. In 1913 a strike by more than 100,000 garment workers began in New York and spread to Boston. The strikers won a reduction of hours, increased wages, and recognition of their union.

Wilson was quickly involved with international problems, first with Mexico and then with Europe. A liberal Mexican government was overthrown in 1913 and General Victoriano Huerta took the presidency. Wilson refused to recognize the Huerta government, despite pressure from U.S. business interests to do so, and announced support for Huerta's opposition. Huerta had won European recognition, however, and the U.S. occupied the port of Veracruz to block delivery of European arms to the Mexican government. War was narrowly averted when Argentina, Brazil, and Chile offered to mediate the dispute. Huerta was forced to resign, and the United States recognized the new Mexican government.

The United States was less fortunate in avoiding war in Europe. In 1914 Germany, Austria, and Turkey went to war with Britain, France, Italy, and Russia, and President Wilson attempted to maintain U.S. neutrality. Attacks on Allied shipping by German submarines resulted in the death of U.S. citizens, and U.S. banks and investors were making loans to the Allies and buying British and French bonds. Allied purchases in the United States created a boom, and railroad and highway construction spurted.

The interception of a telegram from the German foreign secretary, Zimmermann, to the German minister in Mexico helped tip the balance of U.S. opinion against Germany. The note suggested that, should the United States join the Allies, efforts be made to secure an alliance with Mexico, with the promise that parts of Arizona, New Mexico, and Texas would revert to Mexico with a victory by the Central Powers. Publication of the note in the United States in March 1917 followed on the heels of Germany's announcement of the resumption of unrestricted submarine warfare against Allied and neutral shipping.

On April 2, 1917 President Wilson asked congress to declare war on Germany, and on April 6 the president signed the resolution. The United States quickly mobilized, drafting some 3 million men for military service. The U.S. Navy began convoy duty in the Atlantic in May, and in June General John J. Pershing arrived in Paris to direct U.S. land forces, which began to arrive in France two weeks later.

Revolution in Russia had removed that country from the war, and the Central Powers were able to concentrate on their Western Front, against France. But the introduction of fresh troops from the United States, and increased material support from the United States finally helped determine the outcome. The German emperor abdicated, and on November 11, 1918 an armistice was signed.

The peace conference to end what had been the greatest war in modern history was held in Paris, and President Wilson headed the U.S. delegation. Wilson had insisted that it was necessary to establish an international organization to maintain world peace, and the conference agreed to the formation of the League of Nations. In May 1919 the president presented the peace treaty to the U.S. Senate, but the Senate refused to accept the treaty, in large part because it contained the covenant of the League of Nations. Campaigning for support of the treaty, Wilson suffered a stroke and was unable to win the popular backing he felt necessary. On November 19, 1919 the Senate failed to vote for the treaty by the necessary two-thirds majority, and the United States, whose president had led it into being, never joined the League of Nations.

Domestically, the United States entered a strange new period. In October 1919 Congress passed the Volstead Act over President Wilson's veto. The act provided enforcement power for the 18th amendment to the U.S. Constitution, which made the manufacture, sale, transportation, importation, or exportation of alcoholic beverages illegal — Prohibition. A number of states had earlier adopted Prohibition, and it now was the law of the land. Bootleggers and rumrunners, and the speakeasy, became symbols of an era.

The toppling of the monarchy in Russia had been followed by the establishment of a moderate regime in that land, but Communists led by V. I. Ulyanov, better known as Nikolai Lenin, leader of the Bolshevik faction, soon took control. The advent to power of the Bolsheviks in Russia produced apprehension in many parts of the world, and in the United States a "Red scare" led to nationwide arrests and the deportation of more than 200 aliens.

On the eve of the presidential election of 1920, the 19th Amendment to the United States' Constitution was ratified, and women were enfranchised. The election was won decisively by the Republican candidate, Warren G. Harding, but the Socialist candidate, Eugene V. Debs, received close to 1 million votes even though he was in prison on charges of sedition. The Republican victory also ended all hope of the United States joining the League of Nations, but President Wilson had been awarded the 1919 Nobel Peace Prize for his struggle to ensure world peace.

The census of 1920 reported that the population of the United States exceeded 105 million, about a 15 percent increase in a decade, and immigration had accounted for approximately 5.7 million. For the first time in the nation's history, the number of people living in cities was greater than the number living in rural areas.

Under President Harding's leadership, the United States withdrew from the world role it had assumed so short a time before. In his inaugural address he stated, "We seek no part in directing the destinies of the world." And the United States moved to limit immigration, passing the Quota Act in 1921, and to reduce imports, passing the Emergency Tariff Act and other measures in the same year. Unemployment rose sharply as the wartime boom period came to an end, and the Department of Labor estimated that more than 5 million people were without work.

President Harding was taken ill in 1923, and he died on August 2. Vice-President Calvin Coolidge was sworn in as president the following day. His first annual message to Congress, in which he declared his support for a World Court, enforcement of Prohibition, lower taxes, and government economy, was the first official presidential address to be broadcast. Coolidge won election in 1924.

The Coolidge administration was marked by a revival of prosperity in the country, and the exposure of scandals in Washington. Congressional investigators discovered that corruption had been prevalent during Harding's tenure of office, and several of Harding's appointees were found guilty of fraud. The most famous instance was the Teapot Dome Scandal, which involved the Secretary of the Interior accepting a bribe to lease U.S. oil reserves at Teapot Dome, Wyoming, to a private company.

The Coolidge years also saw Richard E. Byrd and Floyd Bennett make the first flight over the North Pole, in 1926, and in 1927 Byrd and three others flew from New York to France to inaugurate official transatlantic airmail service. In that same year, Charles Lindbergh flew alone across the Atlantic from New York to Paris.

President Coolidge refused to run for reelection in 1928, and the Republicans chose Herbert Hoover as their candidate. The Democrats chose New York's governor, Alfred E. Smith, a Roman Catholic. Hoover won the election in a landslide after a campaign that featured Smith's religion as an obstacle to his ability to function freely as preiident.

The prosperity of the Coolidge years came to an abrupt end in 1929, when the New York stock market crashed. A period of unprecedented speculation was over, and the country entered a decade of economic depression. In 1930 President Hoover signed the Smoot-Hawley Tariff, which raised duties to unprecedented heights and led to a sharp drop in international trade. Unemployment had soared, and new restrictions were placed on immigration. Banks failed, and the government moved to inaugurate public works programs.

THE NATION

The Republicans renominated Hoover at their national convention in 1932, and the Democrats again chose a New Yorker, Franklin D. Roosevelt. The depression deepened; unemployment rose to 12 million; banks continued to close; and industry operated at half its 1929 level. Roosevelt promised the nation a program of social reconstruction with government support directed to the "forgotten men," a "new deal" for the individual attempting to survive the economic catastrophe. Hoover reaffirmed his belief in the ability of private enterprise to meet the nation's needs and denounced Roosevelt's program as socialistic.

Roosevelt and the Democratic Party swept to victory in the November elections, winning not only the White House but also almost three-quarters of the House of Representatives and two-thirds of the Senate. Within six months a wide-ranging legislative program had been passed that attempted to meet the critical economic situation and more. And the president took to the radio in a series of broadcasts that became known as fireside chats to explain his programs.

In addition to acts directly relating to stimulating the economy and aiding the destitute, the government launched the Tennessee Valley Authority, a government corporation, to develop the full resources of the Tennessee River Valley, which includes parts of seven states. The TVA was concerned with conservation as well as economic development, and it became a model for similar large-scale development projects in other lands.

New laws made it mandatory that reliable information be made available for all new security issues, and a new banking law guaranteed bank deposits for individuals. Other measures were taken to aid the farmer, the small homeowner, and to spur international trade. Prohibition was ended.

Internationally, the administration established diplomatic relations with the Soviet Union and declared that no nation had the right to interfere in the internal or external affairs of another, a statement directed principally to the American republics. New legislation in 1934 established the Commonwealth of the Philippines, and the islands were assured of independence in 1946.

Roosevelt was reelected in 1936, defeating Republican Alfred Landon and winning the electoral votes of every state but Maine and Vermont. The Democrats also increased their strength in both the House of Representatives and the Senate.

Improvements in the economic and social situation in the United States were soon overshadowed by events in other parts of the world. In Europe, Benito Mussolini headed a Fascist regime in Italy and Adolf Hitler headed a Nazi regime in Germany. Civil war erupted in Spain, in 1936, and the country became a proving ground for World War II in Europe. In Asia, Japan had embarked on a program of territorial expansion, taking control of Manchuria, the extreme northeastern part of China, and seeking to gain control of the rest of that vast nation.

The U.S. Congress reacted to the world crisis by strengthening neutrality legislation in the hope of preventing U.S. involvement. The feeling of the country, still deeply involved in struggling out of economic depression, remained strongly isolationist. President Roosevelt attempted to win support for a "quarantine" of aggressors, but he met with little success.

In 1939 war in Europe seemed imminent. Germany had invaded Czechoslovakia, and Britain and France guaranteed aid to Poland should Germany attack that nation. President Roosevelt had requested funds from Congress to strengthen the U.S. military, but progress had been slow.

War came to Europe in September, when German armies moved across the border with Poland, and Britain and France joined the conflict. The United States declared its neutrality, but the Congress repealed part of the Neutrality Act it had adopted in 1937 and permitted belligerents to purchase war supplies here on a cash-and-carry basis.

Roosevelt was renominated by the Democratic Party in 1940, and Wendell Willkie won the Republican nomination. German armies swept through western Europe — Denmark and Norway; Belgium, Luxemburg, and the Netherlands were all occupied. British troops were forced from the continent, and France was compelled to surrender. The Germans launched massive air attacks against Britain in August 1940, and the Battle of Britain had begun.

Roosevelt won an unprecedented third term as president of the United States, and the Democrats retained control of the Congress. The census of 1940 recorded a population of more than 131 million, but immigration during the preceding decade had been only slightly over 500,000, the lowest figure in more than a century.

In his annual message in January 1941, President Roosevelt enunciated the "four freedoms" that he felt necessary for the postwar world — freedom of speech and expression, freedom of worship, freedom from want, and freedom from fear.

Cooperation with Britain increased, and in March the president signed the Lend-Lease Act, which authorized him to lend war materials to any nation whose defense he felt vital to that of the United States. In May, President Roosevelt declared a national emergency, and in June relations with Germany and Italy were suspended. Germany invaded the Soviet Union on June 22, and Roosevelt pledged U.S. aid to the U.S.S.R.

On December 7, 1941 Japanese airplanes attacked the U.S. Pacific fleet at Pearl Harbor, Hawaii, and on December 8 the congress declared war on Japan. Three days later Germany and Italy, with whom Japan was allied, declared war on the United States, and congress adopted a resolution recognizing that a state of war existed with those countries, too.

The United States rapidly shifted into full economic mobilization. The vast resources of the nation were thrown into the struggle. Japanese forces moved through the Pacific, taking Malaya, Indonesia (then the Netherlands East Indies), and the Philippines. Within the United States, Japanese residents of West Coast states, more than half of whom were U.S.-born citizens, were forcibly removed from their homes and placed in inland relocation camps.

In August 1942 the United States launched its first major offensive against the Japanese, landing U.S. Marines on Guadalcanal, in the Solomon Islands. In November, U.S. forces under the command of General Dwight D. Eisenhower joined the British in landing in North Africa. The country's scientists had begun to work on developing an atomic bomb, for in 1939 Albert Einstein had advised President Roosevelt that Germany was working to develop such a weapon. In September the Manhattan District was formed to direct development, and in December the first controlled, self-sustaining nuclear chain reaction was set off by Enrico Fermi and his co-workers at the University of Chicago.

In 1943 Italy surrendered, and by the end of the year the Allied forces were on the offensive in all areas. On June 6, 1944, D-Day, the Allies launched their invasion of France, and in September U.S. troops entered Germany. Roosevelt was again the Democratic candidate in 1944, and the Republicans nominated Thomas E. Dewey, governor of New York. Roosevelt's vice-presidential candidate was Senator Harry Truman of Missouri. Roosevelt won a fourth term as president of the United States, but on April 12, 1945 he died at Warm Springs, Georgia.

A World Power

Harry Truman succeeded to the presidency and was immediately faced with the formidable tasks of ending the war and securing the peace. On April 25, representatives of 50 nations met in San Francisco to draft the charter of the United Nations, a new international organization to replace the League of Nations. Germany surrendered unconditionally on May 7, after Adolf Hitler had committed suicide, and the war in Europe was over.

Attention turned to the Pacific, and President Truman was faced with a terrible decision. The first atomic bomb had been exploded in the desert at Alamogordo, New Mexico, on July 16, and the Allies had sent an ultimatum to the Japanese government within days of the test. The Japanese rejected the ultimatum, and on August 6, 1945 an atomic bomb was dropped on Hiroshima. A second bomb was dropped on August 9, on Nagasaki, and on August 14 Japan's unconditional surrender had been agreed to.

The U.S. Senate had ratified the Charter of the United Nations almost unanimously in July 1945, and the headquarters of the new world organization were located in the United States. But relations with the Soviet Union deteriorated, and in 1946, speaking at Fulton, Missouri, Winston Churchill declared that an "iron curtain" had descended across the continent of Europe.

Independence was granted the Philippines in 1946, as promised in 1934, and in 1947 the United States undertook to help the war-ravaged nations of Europe through the Marshall Plan, under which some $12 billion dollars in aid was provided for reconstruction.

Truman won the Democratic nomination for president in 1948, and the Republicans again named Thomas E. Dewey their candidate. But the Democratic Party was divided.

Southerners opposed to the party's stand for civil rights for black Americans formed a states' rights party with South Carolina Governor Strom Thurmond as their candidate. And Democrats on the left formed still another party, the Progressive Party, and selected former vice-president and secretary of agriculture Henry Wallace.

Despite all predictions, Harry Truman won the election. In his inaugural address he stressed the importance of the United Nations, the Marshall Plan, and regional security arrangements to the United States.

The 1950s became years of fear for many Americans. The division of the world into two hostile camps, the problems of reverting to a postwar economy, and a Communist victory in China that drove an ally of long standing, Chiang Kai-shek, from the mainland, all contributed to an atmosphere that made possible a new "Red scare." Led by Senator Joseph R. McCarthy, Republican from Wisconsin, the nation plunged into an orgy of charges and counter-charges of treason and subversion.

The United States was again involved in an armed conflict in 1950, when Communist forces of North Korea invaded South Korea, whose government was supported by the United States as part of a world-wide effort to contain the spread of Soviet influence. The U.S. forces, supported by the United Nations, were placed under the command of General Douglas MacArthur, who had commanded U.S. forces in the Pacific during World War II.

The conflict in Korea, in which Communist Chinese forces joined the North Koreans, continued into 1952, when the Republicans nominated as their candidate for president Dwight D. Eisenhower, former supreme commander of Allied forces in Europe, and the Democrats chose Adlai E. Stevenson, Governor of Illinois.

Eisenhower, pledging in his campaign to go to Korea to try to end the conflict, won the election, and Republicans won a majority of seats in both the House of Representatives and the Senate. An armistice was finally signed in Korea on July 27, 1953, but in Congressional elections in 1954, the Democrats won control of both houses of Congress.

Earl Warren, a governor of California and Republican vice-presidential candidate in 1948, was named chief justice of the Supreme Court by President Eisenhower soon after his election, and a new era in U.S. history had begun. On May 17, 1954 the

Supreme Court held in *Brown v. Board of Education of Topeka* that public school segregation was a violation of the 14th Amendment to the Constitution. The decision reversed a ruling of 1896 that had declared "separate but equal" facilities for black and white Americans to be constitutional. Under court orders schools throughout the South where segregation of white and black had been the law, began to integrate their schools, often under the eyes of federal marshals and even troops.

The striking down of the separate-but-equal standard was followed by a resurgence of demands for the full integration of black Americans into all areas of national life. In 1955 a boycott by black riders of segregated city busses in Montgomery, Alabama, led to another decision of the Supreme Court, one forcing desegregation of local transportation facilities. The Reverend Dr. Martin Luther King, Jr., became the leader of the new movement.

President Eisenhower won reelection in 1956, again defeating Adlai Stevenson, but the Democrats won control of both houses of Congress. In 1957 Congress moved for the first time since 1875 to protect the voting rights of black Americans by making it a federal offense to interfere with the right to vote in national elections. And Supreme Court decisions strengthened the rights of citizens under the Bill of Rights.

The world entered the space age in 1957, when the Soviet Union launched an artificial satellite and followed it with a second carrying a dog. A crash program of scientific development was begun in the United States, and the country, long accustomed to thinking of itself as the most technologically advanced nation, began to take stock of its educational resources.

In 1960 the Democrats nominated Senator John F. Kennedy of Massachusetts as their presidential candidate and Senator Lyndon B. Johnson of Texas as the vice-presidential candidate. The Republicans chose Vice-President Richard M. Nixon as their presidential candidate. Kennedy was the first Roman Catholic to seek a presidential nomination since 1928, when Alfred E. Smith ran. The campaign also saw the first televised debates between the two men seeking the presidency. Kennedy won a hairbreadth victory in the election, in which a record vote was recorded.

The population of the United States had passed the 173 million mark by 1960, and almost 70 percent of Americans lived in cities or towns of more than 2500 people.

Immigration during the preceding decade exceeded 2.5 million, and the census recorded that the westward movement of population had continued. The center of population was placed in Illinois.

President Kennedy's inauguration was accompanied by a wave of optimism, especially among younger people. He launched the Peace Corps, which sent many young Americans abroad to work with people in other lands, and he launched the Alliance for Progress, with the goal of providing assistance to the nations of the Western Hemisphere. He pledged to make the United States first in the "Space Race," and he worked to reduce barriers to international trade.

Kennedy's major crisis came in regard to Cuba, where Fidel Castro had come to power and launched a social revolution. The pro-Marxist programs of the Castro government had led to increasing friction with the United States, and thousands of anti-Castro Cubans had found refuge in the United States.

As relations with the United States deteriorated, Castro developed closer ties with the Soviet Union and the Communist bloc of nations. In 1962 President Kennedy announced that the Soviet Union had been building missile installations in Cuba and that the United States would prevent the shipment of offensive weapons to the island. The Soviet Union agreed to remove the weapons it had placed in Cuba, and the crisis ended with a victory for the new administration.

Civil rights demonstrations occurred in many parts of the United States during 1963. In Birmingham, Alabama, troops were brought in to help keep the peace. In August, some 200,000 people from all parts of the nation held a peaceful "March on Washington" to dramatize the national campaign for equality.

On November 22, 1963, John F. Kennedy was assassinated in Dallas, Texas, and Lyndon B. Johnson became the president of the United States. On his arrival in Washington, President Johnson declared that he would follow the policies of his predecessor.

President Johnson won Congressional approval of civil rights legislation stronger than that sought by President Kennedy, and he launched an attack on poverty in the nation. Johnson became the Democratic candidate for president in 1964, and Arizona Senator Barry M. Goldwater was chosen by the Republicans. Johnson won election in his own right by the greatest popular vote in the nation's history, receiving 43 million votes to Goldwater's 27 million.

Civil rights demonstrations continued, and Martin Luther King, awarded the Nobel Peace Prize in 1964, became a national symbol of black America's drive for full participation in the life of the nation. President Johnson continued to press for legislation insuring equal rights and equal opportunities for all Americans, and in 1965 he named Robert C. Weaver to be secretary of housing and urban affairs, bringing the first black American into the cabinet. In 1967 Johnson named the first black justice to the Supreme Court, Thurgood Marshall.

Under the administration of President Johnson, the United States became more deeply involved in a military conflict in Vietnam. U.S. involvement in that area had begun before his administration, and before that of President Kennedy, but U.S. direct participation escalated dramatically. The role of the United States in Southeast Asia became a bitter issue within the country, and demonstrations against the war were to be seen with increasing frequency. The Vietnam war also became the target of many civil rights activists and of those working to eliminate poverty in the United States on the grounds that the nation's resources were being wasted abroad when they were sorely needed at home.

On March 31, 1968 President Johnson announced that he would not seek another term in office, and at the same time he announced a limitation on U.S. bombing of North Vietnam. Vice-President Hubert Humphrey became a candidate for the Democratic nomination, as did Senator Robert F. Kennedy, brother of the slain president.

Martin Luther King, advocate of nonviolence, was assassinated in Memphis, Tennessee, on April 4, 1968, and on May 29, Robert Kennedy was killed in Los Angeles, California. A shocked nation mourned two leaders, and an official investigation into the phenomenon of physical violence in the United States was begun by a commission appointed by President Johnson. But the Congress refused to pass strict gun-control legislation.

The Republican Party once again named Richard M. Nixon as their presidential candidate in 1968, and he chose Maryland's Governor Spiro T. Agnew as his running mate. The Democratic convention, meeting in Chicago and torn by violence and protest, nominated Hubert H. Humphrey. George C. Wallace of Alabama became a candidate of the American Independence Party, which met in Dallas, Texas.

Richard Nixon won a narrow victory over Hubert Humphrey in an election campaign in which the Vietnam conflict was a major issue, but the Democrats won control of the Congress.

President Nixon had announced his intention of "winding down" U.S. participation in the Vietnam war, and in June 1969 he announced the withdrawal of 25,000 U.S. troops as a first step. Further reductions of U.S. military strength in Vietnam were made, and increased emphasis was placed on preparing the South Vietnamese to assume leadership in the struggle against the North Vietnamese under a program of "Vietnamization." But in 1972, after the failure of negotiators meeting in Paris to reach an accord and major North Vietnamese military successes, President Nixon ordered heavy bombing of North Vietnamese transportation links, and the United States mined the harbor of North Vietnam's major port, Haiphong.

The U.S. Space Program had continued under the Nixon administration, and on July 20, 1969 astronaut Neil Armstrong became the first man to set foot on the moon, thus opening a new era in man's history.

Domestically, the president moved to bring inflation under control, and a system of price and wage controls was eventually instituted. But unemployment continued to rise, and the country faced a period of economic recession.

Soon after taking office, President Nixon was faced with the choice of a chief justice of the Supreme Court, and he chose Justice Warren Burger. A few months later another vacancy occurred on the court, but the president's nominee failed to win the approval of the Senate. Gradually however, as vacancies were filled, the court reflected a more conservative position, and the era of the Warren Court came to an end.

Nixon's visits to Red China and his moves to achieve improved relations with that Communist country and with the Soviet Union were generally approved by U.S. voters. In 1972 President Nixon defeated George McGovern, Democrat, in a landslide victory. On January 23, 1973, President Nixon announced that peace with North Vietnam had been achieved.

Before his second election there had been an illegal break-in and wiretapping operation at the Democratic National Headquarters in the Watergate Building in Washington, D.C. As the months went by, administration efforts to conceal the details of this matter became known, and President Nixon was threatened with impeachment. He resigned as president on August 9, 1974.

Spiro Agnew had resigned as vice president in 1973, and President Nixon had appointed Gerald Ford, congressman from Michigan's Fifth District since 1948, to that office. Gerald Ford took office as president of the United States on August 9, 1974. He nominated Nelson A. Rockefeller, former governor of New York, as vice president and Rockefeller assumed that post on December 19, 1974.

During 1974 the nation was experiencing its worst economic depression since the 1930s. President Ford stopped the recession with several successful measures in 1975 and in early 1976 clear signs of recovery became visible. The economy grew at an annual rate of 8.7 per cent in the first quarter of 1976. Construction activity was ahead 13% in comparison to the previous year. For the first five months of 1976 construction starts were valued at $40.65 billion. The threat posed to the environment and to health and safety by continued uncontrolled exploitation of the national resources also drew the attention of many. As they turned to the issue of protecting their natural heritage, they also turned to a fuller appreciation of the·magnificent country. More and more people took to the countryside in autos and campers, on bicycles and on foot, all seeking to explore and to enjoy their land that celebrated its 200th birthday on July 4th, 1976. The third century started with great hopes for continued economic growth and peace.

THE NORTHEAST

MAINE

NEW HAMPSHIRE

VERMONT

MASSACHUSETTS

CONNECTICUT

RHODE ISLAND

NEW YORK

NEW JERSEY

PENNSYLVANIA

THE NORTHEAST

Maine, New Hampshire, Vermont, Massachusetts, Connecticut, Rhode Island, New York, New Jersey, Pennsylvania.

No section of the United States is so inextricably entwined with the early history of the nation and with its economic and cultural ascendancy as the Northeast. It is there that the Pilgrims and Puritans set down roots, that men met to sign the Declaration of Independence and to draft the Constitution, that the first great North American institutions of higher learning were founded, that antislavery agitation was launched.

Although the northeast may no longer play the preeminent political, financial, and cultural role it once did, it nonetheless continues to occupy a vital and powerful place in national life. Its great cities are magnets that attract visitors from all parts of the world. The New York Stock Exchange is a citadel of economic might; the United Nations meets there; scholars and scientists from all over the world come to its universities and research institutes. And although life in its big cities is at times difficult and exhausting, still the cities of the northeast continue to cast a spell. And a wealth of natural beauty lies within reach of those cities — from the isolated salt marshes of the New Jersey coast to the mountains of New Hampshire, from the Finger Lakes of New York to Cape Cod and the rugged Maine coast.

Maine

Settled early in the 1600s by both French and English colonists, Maine became an early battleground in England's struggle against the Indians and the French. The largest of the New England states and the most northeasterly member of the Union, Maine still has large tracts of uninhabited wilderness known only to guides and lumberjacks.

Logging has been Maine's chief industry since colonial times, and some of the state's principal cities — Portland, Bangor, Bath, and Brunswick — originally were lumber ports. Even today, 80 percent of Maine's land is covered with forest. Maine is also famous for the potatoes grown in Aroostock County, a fertile agricultural region near the border with Canada, and for its imcomparable lobsters. Maine's fishing and fish-processing facilities rank among the best in the nation.

It is not surprising that a state with such vast forest preserves, so majestic a coast, and with such an abundance of streams and lakes should be popular with sports enthusiasts and vacationers. Kennebunkport, Ogunquit, York, Bar Harbor, Bethel, Sebago, Casco Bay, Rockland, Castine, Boothbay Harbor, and Mount Desert Island are well-known resorts; skiers flock to Mount Katahdin; and deer, bear, geese, salmon, and trout await the hunter and fisher.

New Hampshire

Even though its coastline is far less extensive and its terrain is more mountainous than the coast and surface of its neighbor to the east, New Hampshire, with its rugged, heavily wooded mountains, magnificent notches, and innumerable lakes and ponds, does resemble Maine.

Most famous of New Hampshire's mountains is the Presidential Range, a part of the White Mountains that contains the state's highest peak, Mt. Washington, with an elevation of more than 6,000 feet. Swift rivers and streams provided water power that helped make New Hampshire a center of manufacturing in the 1800s. The state's stone quarries have long been famous, and New Hampshire is known as the Granite State. Today, in addition to its stone, New Hampshire produces a wide range of products — leather goods, textiles, electrical equipment, and machinery.

Maple sugar, produced from the state's lovely stands of sugar maples, is still a New Hampshire specialty. Fine recreational facilities make the state a popular fishing, hunting, and winter sports area. And the state's scenery, including the lovely Franconia, Sugar Hill, Whitefield, Bretton Woods, Jackson, North Conway, Bethlehem, Pike, Lake Sunapee and Laconia, attracts many tourists. Also the beaches are popular, especially Hampton and Rye Beach.

Vermont

The first European known to have come to Vermont, named for its rolling green hills, was the French explorer Samuel de Champlain. Although the first English settlement did not come into being until 1724, Vermont and its English settlers were destined to play a vital role in the American Revolution. The Green Mountain boys led by

Ethan Allen fought one of the earliest battles of the war, capturing the British fortress Ticonderoga in 1775. Vermont was also the first state to be admitted to the Union after the original thirteen.

The Green Mountains that run through the center of Vermont are a gentle, lovely range, but the state's poor, rocky soil posed a formidable problem for the early settlers. Because it is neither a good agricultural area nor greatly industrialized, Vermont is the least populated of the northeastern states. It is, however, a major producer of granite, marble, lumber, pulp, and dairy products. And Vermont is famous for its fine skiing, lovely lakes, state parks and forests, and its picturesque towns and villages.

Massachusetts

Although Europeans may have reached what is now Massachusetts earlier, the area was not settled until the arrival of the Pilgrims in 1620. The Mayflower compact drawn up by these first settlers stands as a remarkable document of self-government. The Pilgrims and the Puritans, who arrived soon after, left their mark not only on the territory to which they came but on all of American life. Their ethic of work shaped the course of Massachusetts and the other New England states. Their descendants became the leaders of the new nation's political, economic and cultural life; the statesmen and jurists, the merchants and writers. They helped draft the laws of the land, founded universities and banking institutions, and processed and sold the raw materials of all parts of the nation.

In the mid-1800s a new wave of immigrants began to pour into Massachusetts — Irish victims of famine, Italians, Poles, Lithuanians, Scandinavians, Germans, East European Jews, and Portuguese. All sought a more secure and better life and in the course of time achieved a measure of success. Their children, particularly the offspring of the Irish and Italian immigrants, are today found among the powerful political and economic leaders of the nation.

Massachusetts is not only the historically important citadel of the Puritan ethic, the home of the Adamses and Cabots and Lodges, of Emily Dickinson and of Thoreau, but also a land of delightful old towns, superb ocean resorts, and lovely green mountains. Boston, its capital city, the scene of the famous Tea Party in 1773 that helped

51

spark the American Revolution, is an important port and justly famous for its historic monuments, symphony orchestra, museums, and schools. Nearby Cambridge houses two of America's most famous institutions of higher learning, Harvard University and the Massachusetts Institute of Technology (MIT). Wood's Hole is the site of a renowned scientific research center; Provincetown on Cape Cod is famous for its artists' colony; and summer music and dance festivals make the Berkshires a popular vacation area.

Connecticut

One of the original thirteen states, Connecticut was first settled by the Dutch in 1633. Soon after, dissident members of Massachusetts' Plymouth Colony also came to Connecticut and set up a trading post on the Connecticut River. Today Connecticut is a thriving industrial and commercial state, and the fertile valley of the Connecticut River is a well-developed agricultural area.

Hartford, the capital of the state, is a major manufacturing community as well as the headquarters for many of the nation's insurance companies, whose combined assets run into the billions of dollars. Yale University, one of America's most distinguished educational institutions, is located at New Haven. Long Island Sound has long been a favorite with fishing and boating enthusiasts, and the lovely countryside within commuting distance of New York City contains some of the most prosperous suburban communities of the eastern United States.

Rhode Island

Rhode Island was settled by nonconformists who left Massachusetts in search of religious and political tolerance. Prominent among these was Roger Williams, who established the first settlement at Providence, the present state capital, in 1636.

Although Rhode Island is heavily industrialized, two-thirds of its land is still uncultivated woodland and forest. Dairying and poultry farming are its chief agricultural activities. The state's shallow coastal waters abound in shellfish, particularly the quahaug clam, one of Rhode Island's most famous food products.

Providence is a manufacturing center for machinery, plastics, jewelry, electrical equipment, and rubber goods. It is also the site of Brown University, one of the country's oldest institutions of higher education. Nearby Newport, long one of the nation's wealthiest and most fashionable seaside resorts, achieved more recent fame as host to an annual summer jazz festival.

New York

The first European to sight New York may well have been an Italian, Giovanni de Verrazano, in 1524. Almost a century later Henry Hudson, an Englishman in the employ of a Dutch company, explored the river that now bears his name. In 1626 Dutch colonists headed by Peter Minuit purchased Manhattan Island from the Indians, and by 1643 the island had a multilingual population of 500 inhabitants. The city has retained its cosmopolitan character to this day, but now the population of New York City and its environs amounts to more than 11 million.

New York is a state of contrasts, with great urban and industrial centers, a fertile river valley containing farms and orchards, rich vineyards, woodlands, mountains, and beautiful lakes.

New York City, a fascinating, vibrant metropolis, with towering buildings, noisy streets, rushing crowds, busy airports and docks, is the headquarters of the country's garment and fashion industries, of publishing and advertising, of its theater, art, musical, and financial life. There the United Nations meets in a striking building overlooking the East River. Albany, the state capital, was originally a Dutch fur-trading post. Buffalo, an important inland port on Lake Erie and the second-largest city in the state, is linked to Canada by bridge and to New York City by a waterway. Niagara Falls, on the border with Canada, is a traditional mecca for honeymooners. Rochester, lying in one of the richest truck-gardening and fruit-growing sections of the country, is also the home of the world's largest manufacturers of films and cameras.

Pennsylvania

Toward the end of the 1600s, William Penn, a Quaker, established a colony for people of all religious beliefs in Pennsylvania, a region originally settled by the Swedes in 1638. Soon afterward other persecuted groups seeking a freer life, such as Mennonites and Moravians from Central Europe, also arrived. But the English Quakers long remained the dominant group.

Pennsylvania is one of the states that successfully combines the old with the new, agriculture with industry. Although rich in minerals — coal and oil — and thus the home of related industries, it still has large unspoiled areas, particularly in the Piedmont Plateau, covered by deciduous forests. And the farms in fertile southeastern Pennsylvania make the state a significant agricultural producer.

For more than a century anthracite coal dominated the life of northeastern Pennsylvania, but as other fuels began to replace coal in industrial society, the region became depressed. In an effort to achieve some measure of economic stability, Pennsylvania has encouraged the development of light industry in the region, and today it enjoys a fair degree of prosperity.

Philadelphia, the city of Brotherly Love, the seat of the two Continental congresses, has seen a renaissance since World War II. This once elegant, wealthy city had deteriorated alarmingly until, by 1940, it was marked by sprawling, dreary slums. But today Philadelphia is well on its way to becoming a model of urban planning and revitalization. The historic treasures of the nation have been the focus of a great restoration program, and continue to attract many tourists each year.

The battle of Gettysburg, in which the Confederates suffered a decisive defeat, marked a turning point in the U.S. Civil War. And it was at the site of this great battle that President Abraham Lincoln delivered one of the most stirring addresses of the nation's history — his Gettysburg Address.

Pittsburgh, in western Pennsylvania, is a great industrial center, the producer of much of America's iron and steel. Not too long ago the city was all but invisible, blanketed with smoke and soot. Today most of the noxious smog has been eliminated and handsome buildings mark the downtown center.

New Jersey

The New Jersey seashore probably has been host to more sunbathers per square foot of sand than any other beach area anywhere in the world. In addition, New Jersey has a large and varied group of industries and is a major producer of vegetables, poultry, and dairy products. The combination of sea and sand, agriculture and industry has helped make New Jersey one of the most densely populated states of the Union.

Newark, a major manufacturing center and seaport, is also the site of many small workshops and important research laboratories. It is also an important center of the insurance industry. Jersey City, the state's second-largest city and linked to New York City by tunnel, is both a manufacturing center and a port. Princeton, a lovely pre-Revolutionary town, is the home of prestigious Princeton University and of the world-famed Institute for Advanced Study, which has served as a haven for some of the world's most renowned scholars, among them Albert Einstein. Princeton also was the scene of a famous battle of the Revolutionary War in which General George Washington defeated the English in 1777. Trenton, the state capital, and Monmouth were other important battlesites of that war, and George Washington delivered his farewell address to his armies at Rocky Hill. The best known of New Jersey's many ocean-front resorts, Atlantic City, is still popular with sponsors of political and commercial conventions and is famous as the site of the annual Miss America beauty pageant.

The NORTHEAST
Description of the following pictures

page 57   NEW YORK HARBOR
STATUE OF LIBERTY, NEW YORK HARBOR

The most famous statue in the world stands on Liberty Island in the upper bay of New York Harbor, welcoming every visitor to the United States who arrives by sea. She was created by the French sculptor Frédéric Auguste Bartholdi, who portrayed Liberty stepping free of broken chains, holding a torch high in her right hand and cradling in her left arm a tablet representing the Declaration of Independence. The statue is 151 feet tall and stands on a pedestal 154 feet high. The top of the torch is more than 300 feet above the ground. The cost of the statue was met through thousands of small donations by the people of France. The Statue of Liberty represented a gift of friendship in the truest sense.

LOWER MANHATTAN

This air view from Brooklyn over Government Island to Lower Manhattan shows clearly the extent of New York Harbor. The tall building in Lower Manhattan surpassing all others in height is the new World Trade Center. It has on its roof the highest observatory in the world, open to the public.

MORNING IN THE HARBOR

An early morning view with the sun far to the east shows the famous skyline of Lower Manhattan, and to the right the mouth of the East River emptying into New York harbor, with Brooklyn Bridge clearly visible.

page 58   NEW YORK CITY
WORLD TRADE CENTER

New York's newest landmark is in the heart of the oldest part of the city, surrounded by historical buildings and points of interest such as Federal Hall, where George Washington was inaugurated, Castle Clinton National Monument, Trinity Church, Wall Street, City Hall, Statue of Liberty and many more. The Trade Center comprises twin towers, each 110 stories high. It is a city in itself, with many shops, banks, restaurants, offices, railroads, subway trains and landscaped plazas. There is an acre of space on every floor in each tower, with 43,600 windows and 600,000 square feet of glass.
Clearly visible in the photograph is the promenade deck on the roof above the 110th floor of the left tower. It is 1,377 feet up in the sky, highest outdoor observation platform in the world. The view from there is unique.

(continued on page 73)

STATUE OF LIBERTY

LOWER MANHATTAN

NEW YORK HARBOR

MORNING IN THE HARBOR

WORLD TRADE CENTER

NEW YORK CITY

VIEW FROM THE OBSERVATORY
OF THE WORLD TRADE CENTER

ROCKEFELLER CENTER
LOWER PLAZA

UNITED NATIONS
HEADQUARTERS →

58

ST. PATRICK'S
CATHEDRAL

RCA BUILDING
ROCKEFELLER
CENTER

CENTRAL PARK SOUTH

**NEW YORK
CITY**

PARK AVENUE

*METROPOLITAN
OPERA HOUSE
LINCOLN CENTER*

**NEW YORK
CITY**

*GEORGE WASHINGTON
BRIDGE*

HUDSON VALLEY FROM BEAR MOUNTAIN

*NIAGARA
FALLS*

**NEW YORK
STATE**

MONTAUK POINT
LIGHTHOUSE
LONG ISLAND

62

DUNES AT PROVINCETOWN
MASSACHUSETTS

WHERE THE
PILGRIMS LANDED

PLYMOUTH ROCK,
PLYMOUTH, MASS.

BASS RIVER,
CAPE COD

MASSACHUSETTS

**WHERE THE VIKINGS
VISITED, 1000 A.D.**

*GAY HEAD
MARTHA'S VINEYARD*

64

BOSTON'S CENTER: THE COMMON AND PUBLIC GARDEN

MASSACHUSETTS

THE STATE HOUSE

**BOSTON
MASSACHUSETTS**

*DOORWAY ON
BEACON STREET*

HARVARD UNIVERSITY
CAMBRIDGE

MASSACHUSETTS

GRANARY BURYING
GROUND AND
PARK STREET CHURCH

NUBBLE LIGHT, YORK, MAINE

THE COVE, OGUNQUIT, MAINE

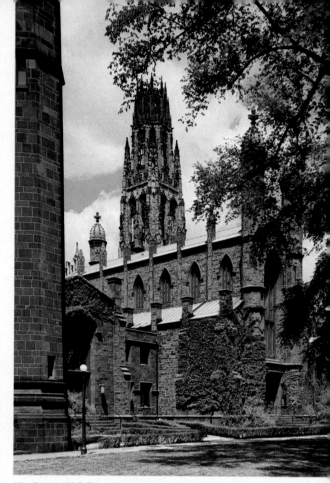

YALE UNIVERSITY, NEW HAVEN, CONNECTICUT

STATE CAPITOL, HARTFORD, CONNECTICUT

NEW ENGLAND

MOUNT WASHINGTON, NEW HAMPSHIRE

FALL IN NEW HAMPSHIRE, WHITEFIELD

WINTER IN VERMONT: MT. MANSFIELD

THE BERKSHIRES, NEW ASHFORD, MASS.

INDEPENDENCE HALL, PHILADELPHIA, PENNSYLVANIA

70

*NATIONAL
HISTORICAL PARK
MORRISTOWN*

NEW JERSEY

*PALMER SQUARE
PRINCETON*

Description of foregoing pictures —
continued from page 56

page 58   NEW YORK STATE

VIEW FROM THE OBSERVATORY OF THE WORLD TRADE CENTER

This is the view down to the south, high over the skyscrapers, deep into the canyons of the streets of the oldest part of New York. Battery Park and Government Island are visible, and also, to the left, some piers of Brooklyn. On clear days the views in all directions are about unlimited. To the north is a beautiful view all over Manhattan, up to George Washington Bridge over the Hudson, Queensboro and Triboro bridges, over the East River. To the east, looking over Brooklyn and Long Island, the airports may be clearly seen. To the west almost the whole state of New Jersey can be scanned over the Hudson River. The south opens a unique view over New York Harbor to Staten Island, the Statue of Liberty, Verrazano Narrows Bridge, into the Atlantic Ocean and the coast of New Jersey.

ROCKEFELLER CENTER, LOWER PLAZA

In front of the RCA Building is a large open court set some two stories below street level. This Lower Plaza is dominated by a golden statue of Prometheus by Paul Manship and is flanked by the flags of many nations. The plaza serves a variety of purposes. Here a

Salvation Army band is shown giving a concert. In winter, ice skaters glide by the window-walls of two restaurants, which in summer serve meals and drinks at umbrella-shaded tables.

page 59   NEW YORK CITY

ST. PATRICK'S CATHEDRAL

New York's Roman Catholic cathedral, St. Patrick's, stands on Fifth Avenue opposite Rockefeller Center. It was begun in 1858 and completed some 20 years later. It was the first cathedral to be built in Gothic Revival Style in the United States. The exterior design is based on that of Germany's Cologne Cathedral, and its interior, with its long nave and high central vault, derives directly from France's Amiens Cathedral.

UNITED NATIONS HEADQUARTERS

The headquarters buildings of the United Nations occupy the southern half of a beautifully landscaped plot extending along the East River from 42nd to 48th streets in Manhattan. The 39-story Secretariat Building towers over the site. Its broad east and west walls are made up of 5,400 blue-green glass windows set in aluminum frames. The north and south walls are of Vermont marble.

TOMB OF THE UNKNOWN SOLDIER OF THE REVOLUTION, WASHINGTON SQUARE, PHILADELPHIA, PENNSYLVANIA

←

ROCKEFELLER CENTER, THE RCA BUILDING

Rockefeller Center was the first large modern office complex to be built in New York City. Fourteen buildings were put up in the 1930s on a plot of land between 48th and 51st streets and between Fifth Avenue and the Avenue of the Americas. Other buildings were added later. The 70-story RCA Building is the tallest. On top of it is the famous Rainbow Room, a popular restaurant and cocktail lounge. The RCA Building is flanked by twin seven-story buildings, the Maison Française and the British Empire Building.

page 60   NEW YORK CITY

CENTRAL PARK SOUTH

Central Park, with more than 800 acres in the center of Manhattan, has many areas that retain the original ruggedness of the island's terrain and gives an indication of what the area looked like before the city covered it. Playgrounds, zoos, athletic fields, bridle paths and lakes are among the park's facilities. Concerts of classical and popular music and the plays of Shakespeare are presented free during the summer. This photo shows the southern part of the park, with some skyscrapers on Fifth Avenue (left) and the Plaza Hotel to the right.

PARK AVENUE

It is the city's widest and most fashionable street. The photograph shows in the background the Pan American Building, to the left part of the Waldorf-Astoria Hotel, to the right office buildings between 51st and 45th streets. Under the street run the tracks of the New York Central and New Haven Railroads. The Pan American Building is an octagonal giant, 59 stories high, and has 2,400,000 square feet of office space, housing more than 25,000 workers.

page 61   NEW YORK CITY

LINCOLN CENTER, METROPOLITAN OPERA

On the west side of Manhattan is glittering Lincoln Center, a complex of splendid buildings designed for music, theater, and dance. Included in the group is the new Metropolitan Opera House. The dancing fountain in the center provides a beautiful introduction to the world of opera in New York City. The two murals shown within the left and right arches of the Metropolitan are the work of Marc Chagall. The sparkling chandelier was a gift of the Austrian government.

GEORGE WASHINGTON BRIDGE

Looking south over the Hudson from the New Jersey side, the picture shows the George Washington Bridge and under it the skyline of Manhattan. One of the most graceful bridges in all America, it connects Upper Manhattan at 178th street with Fort Lee, New Jersey, by a span that is almost a mile long. The only

New York City bridge over the Hudson River, it was built in 1931 by O. H. Amman and Cass Gilbert.

page 62   NEW YORK STATE
NIAGARA FALLS
The Niagara River, which forms the border between New York State and Canada, supplies the tremendous sheet of water that drops about 190 feet over the falls — more than 3000 feet in width. There are really two falls, separated by Goat Island. The U.S. portion is 1075 feet wide and the Canadian falls 2200 feet wide. The falling waters average three feet in depth. Close by is the city of Niagara Falls. The falls are one of the most popular U.S. tourist attractions.

HUDSON VALLEY, VIEW FROM BEAR MOUNTAIN
One of the most popular recreational areas in the Hudson Valley is Bear Mountain, a 1000-acre park that is part of Palisades Interstate Park. Bear Mountain itself rises to an elevation of more than 1300 feet and offers a beautiful view of the Hudson Valley.

MONTAUK POINT LIGHTHOUSE, LONG ISLAND
At the eastern end of Long Island, and the easternmost point of New York State, stands Montauk Point Lighthouse, built in 1795. Nearby is the town of Montauk, a popular summer resort and a favorite port of deep-sea fishermen.

page 63   WHERE THE PILGRIMS LANDED
THE DUNES AT PROVINCETOWN, CAPE COD, MASSACHUSETTS
In November 1620, the Pilgrims landed at Provincetown, which lies on the northern tip of Cape Cod in southeastern Massachusetts. Just behind the town are magnificent sand dunes heaped up by Atlantic storms. The soft sands shifting before the wind are a singular sight. The area is now part of Cape Cod National Seashore.

PLYMOUTH ROCK, PLYMOUTH, MASSACHUSETTS
The monument in the harbor of Plymouth stands over famous Plymouth Rock, where the Pilgrims finally went ashore in December 1620 to found the first permanent European settlement in New England. A national shrine, it is visited by thousands of people each year.

page 64   MASSACHUSETTS
BASS RIVER, CAPE COD, MASSACHUSETTS
This aerial view shows an interesting part of Cape Cod. Here is where Vikings may well have landed in about 1000 A.D. and stayed the winter. The Bass River is visible in the foreground, and Grand Cove and Nantucket Sound can be glimpsed in the background.

MARTHA'S VINEYARD, GAY HEAD
Another area associated with the Vikings is the colorful island of Martha's Vineyard,

75

which lies about six miles south of Cape Cod. The varicolored cliffs of Gay Head are at the western end of the island. The island has fine harbors and a seafaring tradition that goes back to the days of the New England whalers. There are also fine beaches, and today Martha's Vineyard is a popular resort.

MASSACHUSETTS
BOSTON'S CENTER, THE COMMON AND PUBLIC GARDEN
From the observatory of the John Hancock Building a beautiful view opens over the center of Boston, with the Public Garden in the foreground and, just beyond it, the Common and the State House. The group of three large buildings in the background is the new Government Center, containing city, state, and federal offices.

page 66   BOSTON, MASS.
THE STATE HOUSE
Situated on a hill overlooking the Boston Common and Public Garden, the Massachusetts State House was built in 1795 on land bought from John Hancock. It was designed by Charles Bulfinch. In its Archives Museum are the Charter of the Massachusetts Bay Company of 1628 and the State Constitution of 1780.

DOORWAY ON BEACON STREET
Beacon Street, in the heart of the oldest part of Boston, is lined with many elegant old homes.

page 67   MASSACHUSETTS
HARVARD UNIVERSITY, CAMBRIDGE
Harvard, founded in 1636, is the oldest college in the United States. It is located in Cambridge, not far from Boston. The photo shows part of the historic Yard with Massachusetts Hall, built in 1720.

GRANARY BURYING GROUND AND PARK STREET CHURCH
Three signers of the Declaration of Independence are buried in this historic graveyard — Samuel Adams, John Hancock, and Robert Treat Paine. It is also the final resting place of Paul Revere, Peter Faneuil, and Benjamin Franklin's parents. The Park Street Church, shown to the right, was built in the early 1800s and was the site of William Lloyd Garrison's anti-slavery address of 1829.

page 68   NEW ENGLAND
NUBBLE LIGHT, YORK, MAINE
This view of the Nubble Light near York, which was settled in 1630, shows a typical stretch of Maine's rocky coast.

THE COVE, OGUNQUIT, MAINE
One of the many beautiful resorts along the Maine coast is Ogunquit, which has a three-mile-long sandy beach and good hotels. Ogunquit was named by the original inhabitants of the region, the Natick Indians, and means "beautiful place by the sea."

YALE UNIVERSITY, NEW HAVEN, CONNECTICUT

Yale, named for a generous patron, Elihu Yale, was chartered in 1701. In 1716 classes were moved to the present campus in New Haven. In the center of Memorial Quadrangle is the towering Harkness Tower.

THE STATE CAPITOL, HARTFORD, CONNECTICUT

The attractive marble and granite state house on Hartford's Capitol Hill was designed by Richard Upjohn in 1878. In addition to state offices, it contains an interesting collection of materials relating to Connecticut's history.

page 69   NEW ENGLAND

MOUNT WASHINGTON, NEW HAMPSHIRE

The highest peak in the White Mountains and in New England, stately 6000-foot Mt. Washington dominates northern New Hampshire. A cog railway from Bretton Woods and an automobile toll road lead up to its summit, which offers a magnificent view of the surrounding valleys and mountains.

FALL IN NEW HAMPSHIRE, WHITEFIELD

The fall coloring of the trees, especially the maples, is excitingly beautiful in New England, and this scene in northern New Hampshire is typical of the entire area.

Toward the end of September, after early frosts, Indian Summer brings warmer weather and creates a sunny and brilliant autumn season that lasts until the end of October.

WINTER IN NEW ENGLAND

The New England states, especially Massachusetts, Vermont, and New Hampshire, are famous for their winter sports resorts. Two of the best known winter resort areas are Stowe, in Vermont, and the Berkshires.

page 70   PHILADELPHIA

INDEPENDENCE HALL, PHILADELPHIA, PA.

Begun in 1732 as the State House of the Province of Pennsylvania, the hall became the headquarters of the American Revolution and the meeting place of the founding fathers of the nation. In this building the Declaration of Independence was signed, and there the Second Continental Congress met in 1775 and decided to resist England. In the Assembly Room are the ink stand used for the signing of the Declaration of Independence and the chair occupied by George Washington during the drafting of the Constitution.

page 71   NEW JERSEY

MORRISTOWN, NATIONAL HISTORICAL PARK

The photo shows the grounds surrounding the Ford Mansion, part of the National Historical Park at Morristown, New Jersey. The house was built in the 1770s by Col. Jacob Ford, Jr., and is in perfect condition. It contains many mementos and furnishings of the Ford family and materials relating to the Revolutionary War and to George Washington, who lived in the house during the winter of 1779-1780. Nearby were the encampments of the Continental Army.

PRINCETON, PALMER SQUARE

Princeton, New Jersey, home of one of the oldest and most respected universities in the United States, maintains a historic dignity. One of the major battles of the Revolutionary War took place there in 1777, and in 1783 the Continental Congress met in Princeton's Nassau Hall, making the town the temporary capital of the new country. George Washington lived nearby during much of that time, and it was there that he delivered his famous farewell to his troops.

page 72   PENNSYLVANIA

PHILADELPHIA, WASHINGTON SQUARE

Designed by William Penn, Washington Square is one of the original squares of Philadelphia. In 1706 it became a public burial ground and during the Revolutionary War thousands of unknown soldiers of Washington's army were buried there. The beautiful memorial erected as a tribute to the unknown soldier of the Revolution has an excellent statue of George Washington in the center.

THE SOUTH

WASHINGTON, D.C.

DELAWARE

MARYLAND

VIRGINIA

WEST VIRGINIA

KENTUCKY

NORTH CAROLINA

SOUTH CAROLINA

TENNESSEE

GEORGIA

ALABAMA

MISSISSIPPI

FLORIDA

LOUISIANA

TEXAS

OKLAHOMA

ARKANSAS

PUERTO RICO

VIRGIN ISLANDS

THE SOUTH

Washington, D.C., Delaware, Maryland, Virginia, West Virginia, Kentucky, North Carolina, South Carolina, Tennessee, Georgia, Alabama, Mississippi, Florida, Louisiana, Texas, Oklahoma, Arkansas —
— and Puerto Rico and the Virgin Islands

Unlike the Northeast, the South long remained predominantly agricultural. The climate in the plains extending from the coast to the Appalachians is warmer and the land more fertile. Yet the South is known not only for its farmers and its elegant plantations, but also for its frontiersmen, men like Davy Crockett, who ventured into unexplored territories and who helped blaze the trails that opened up new lands to the west.

The old southern agricultural economy rested heavily on slavery, and many thousands of Africans were brought to the South to work the rich land. But not every Southerner was a slave owner or even sympathetic to slave-owning. At the time of the Civil War, for example, four southern states — Delaware, Kentucky, Maryland, and what is now West Virginia — did not secede from the Union.

The South, again unlike the Northeast, was settled for the most part not by victims of religious persecution but by men and women in search of more land and a better life than England of the 1600s had to offer them. Later, in the 1700s, religious conflicts in Scotland set off a new wave of emigration. Many of these Scots eventually made their way to the New World and settled in the Piedmont Plateau, west of the Virginia and North Carolina Tidewater country. They farmed industriously and brought up their children to believe that "The Lord helps those who help themselves."

The defeat it suffered in the Civil War left the South beaten economically, bitter in spirit, and dreaming of a past that never really existed. But with the passage of time came hope, and with hope the energy to rebuild. Later, in the 1930s during the New Deal era, came vast undertakings such as the Tennessee Valley Authority (TVA), which brought electricity to wide areas and provided a potent stimulus to economic growth. The World War II years and the decades of the 1950s and 1960s saw major changes in all areas of Southern life. Cotton has largely been abandoned as the dominant crop, especially in the areas east of Mississippi. Fields are now being given over to vegetable crops or to pasture. Large industrial centers have arisen, and cities such as Atlanta are major national commercial and financial centers.

The New South is more than factories, offices, and banks. Old myths of black and white are giving way, painfully and slowly, perhaps, and new patterns of life are emerging. And Southern leaders can be heard calling for an end to segregation and discrimination.

Washington, D.C.

The 67-square-mile District of Columbia, lying on the border between the North and the South, was chosen as the site of the nation's capital because it was then approximately at the center of the nation — halfway between Vermont and Georgia. Although it is in a border zone, Washington has a Southern flavor.

Located on three rivers, the Potomac, the Anacostia, and Rock Creek, Washington may well be the handsomest city in the United States. Built according to plans originally drawn up by Pierre Charles L'Enfant in 1791, it is a city of broad boulevards, gracious parks, and splendid vistas. The view of downtown Washington from the Capitol is truly enchanting. To the west stretches the Mall, with the towering Washington Monument, and beyond lie the Reflecting Pool and the Lincoln Memorial. The White House is to the north of the Capitol, and the Jefferson Memorial is to the south.

As the seat of the Federal government Washington deals with the problems of the entire nation, yet it has been unable to solve many of its own local problems. The majority of the city's permanent residents are black, and many of these people are poor and wretchedly housed. The powerful men of Washington thus face the unresolved problems that afflict major cities throughout the country.

Lawmakers, lawyers, lobbyists, civil servants, and members of foreign diplomatic staffs are the people who make the wheels go round in Washington. The ceremonials of office and of tradition give the city much of its color. Washington is also the home of the great Library of Congress, the Smithsonian Institution, and five universities. The splendid National Gallery of Art has one of the world's finest collections, and the new Kennedy Center has stimulated the performing arts. All of these attractions combine to make Washington one of the nation's principal tourist centers.

Delaware

The first Europeans to settle in Delaware were Dutch and Swedes, who arrived in the 1600s. Delaware was one of the thirteen original states, and was the first to ratify the Federal constitution.

The second smallest in area of the 50 states, Delaware lies on the coastal plain along the Atlantic. The entire state is on the Delmarva Peninsula, a fertile plain divided among three states: Delaware *(Del)*, Maryland *(mar)*, and Virginia *(va)*. Although an important producer of vegetables and poultry, and a major processor of seafood, Delaware is an industrial and commercial state whose economic life is associated with one of the world's mightiest industrial empires — Du Pont.

Wilmington, founded by the early Dutch and Swedish settlers, is an important manufacturing and shipping center and the state's most populous city. The town green of Dover, the state capital, was laid out in 1717. It is one of the many points of historical interest to be found in Delaware. And the state's eastern shore has magnificent, wide beaches.

Maryland

The first European settlement in Maryland was established in 1634 by George Calvert, Lord Baltimore. Maryland was founded on the principle of religious tolerance, and the state has played a significant role in the nation's history. In the 1760s a long-standing border dispute with Pennsylvania was settled by the drawing of the Mason-Dixon line. In the War of 1812, it was from the battlements of Fort McHenry that Francis Scott Key saw, by the rockets' red glare and the bombs bursting in air, that the Star Spangled Banner was still there.

Chesapeake Bay, which divides Maryland's coastal plain, has been an important commercial artery since the first days of the nation. The bay is also renowned for its commercial and sports fishing, and for its oysters, crabs, and clams. Baltimore, a major port and industrial center on Chesapeake Bay, is also the home of the Johns Hopkins University. Annapolis, the state capital, is the site of the U.S. Naval Academy and of St. John's University. The city has preserved its eighteenth century waterfront and many of its charming Colonial buildings. Bethesda and Chevy Chase are suburbs of Washington, D.C.

Marylanders have loved horses for two centuries, and the state's major race tracks are known throughout the nation. Asateague Island, straddling Maryland and Virginia, is the home of the concoteague wild ponies, descendants of horses shipwrecked there hundreds of years ago. The Eastern Shore, a region of farms and delightful old towns, is famous for its boating and fishing. In the western part of the state, in the fringes of the Alleghenies, skiing is rapidly gaining in popularity.

Virginia

Perhaps no other state of the Union is so identified with the early history of the United States as the "Old Dominion," as Virginia is known. Named for Elizabeth I, the Virgin Queen, Virginia was the site of the first successful English colony, Jamestown; founded in 1607. In Tidewater Virginia the descendants of those early English settlers — gentlemen adventurers, yeomen, laborers, convicts — developed a gracious and elegant society based on the wealth derived from tobacco. Today something of this world can be seen at Williamsburg, a faithful and evocative restoration of the past. Early in the 1700s, Scots migrated to Virginia and opened its western reaches — the Piedmont, Blue Ridge, and Appalachian regions.

Virginians were among the first leaders of the United States — George Washington, Thomas Jefferson, James Madison. They helped lead its armies and write its basic documents. In the mid-1800s, during the era of disunion and the Civil War, Virginia's capital, Richmond, became the capital of the confederacy, and Virginia was one of the major battlegrounds of the war. And Virginians again were among the leaders. Robert E. Lee, commander of the Confederate military, is still revered although he was forced to surrender at Appomattox in 1865.

Virginia today is much more than fine old mansions and historic battlefields, however. The state continues to be an important agricultural producer, and Richmond is one of the great tobacco markets. It is also a significant producer of manufactured goods, and the Norfolk Naval Shipyard at Hampton Roads is one of the oldest and most important naval repair stations in the country. The Port of Hampton Roads, which includes the harbors of Newport News, Norfolk, and Portsmouth, is a major Atlantic port of the United States. Northern Virginia includes some of the most elegant suburbs of Washington, D.C.

Virginia is also a center of tourism. In addition to such popular sites as Williamsburg, Washington's home, Mount Vernon, and Jefferson's home, Monticello, attract many thousands of visitors each year.

West Virginia

Settled largely by rugged pioneers who had made their way across the Appalachian Mountains, West Virginia had little in common with the rest of Virginia. Few were slaveholders and few supported the movement for secession that preceded the Civil War. In 1861 the region declared its independence of the rest of Virginia and joined the Union as West Virginia.

Coal lies under some two-thirds of West Virginia, and the state produces natural gas. But today many areas have been stripped of coal, and many poor, unemployed miners have been left behind. But manufacturing has increased, especially in the Ohio Valley. The state's industries produce metals and chemicals, and West Virginia is known for its fine glassware. Large herds of dairy and beef cattle are raised in the bluegrass region of the southeast.

Millions of acres of beautiful land are reserved for recreation. And the state's many mineral springs, notably White Sulphur Springs and Berkeley Springs, have long been favorite vacation retreats.

Kentucky

Settled by the English in the mid-1770s, Kentucky was the site of bloody wars among American Indian tribes. Those struggles gave the state the name of the "Dark and Bloody Ground." In the later 1700s, settlers began to flow into the region through the Cumberland Gap. Today Kentucky is best known as the land of Daniel Boone, thoroughbred horses, and Kentucky whiskey. The state's fertile land produces valuable crops, and its famous pastures support rich herds of cattle and prized horses. Kentucky also has rich deposits of minerals.

Lexington, in the Bluegrass region, is the center of horse breeding. And Louisville is the home of the Kentucky Derby, run annually at Churchill Downs. Louisville also produces about a quarter of the whiskey distilled in the United States. Frankfort, the state capital, is also rich in distilleries. Mammoth Cave, one of the finest cave complexes in the United States, is a major tourist attraction.

North Carolina

One of the first states to be settled by the English, North Carolina played an important role in the American Revolution. In 1775 North Carolinians met in Mecklenburg and drew up the Mecklenburg Declaration, which contained phrases resembling those of the Declaration of Independence of 1776. North Carolina also has the oldest state university in the United States, at Chapel Hill, opened in 1795.

North Carolina is a truly beautiful region, from the magnificent beaches of the Outer Banks on the Atlantic westward to the Great Smoky Mountains. Kitty Hawk, on the Outer Banks, a string of islands lining the 300-mile North Carolina coast, was the site of the Wright Brothers' historic flight. Nearby is the birthplace of Virginia Dare, the first English child to be born in America. Cape Hatteras, with its towering lighthouse, is an Atlantic site. The Great Smokies dominate the western part of the state. There, on a reservation, live some 3000 Cherokee Indians, the descendants of the most powerful Indian nation of the South.

Between the Outer Banks and the Great Smokies lie farms and pastures, timber stands and industrial complexes, and prosperous and charming cities. Charlotte, the largest city in the state, is a manufacturing and trucking center. Winston-Salem, North Carolina's industrial center, is a major producer of tobacco products. Raleigh, the state capital, is the commercial hub of a rich tobacco region. Nearby Durham is the home of Duke University. Asheville, at the entrance to the Great Smokies, was founded in the late 1700s and has long been a popular resort. It is the birthplace of the novelist Thomas Wolfe, who celebrated the city in his autobiographical *Look Homeward, Angel.*

South Carolina

The first Europeans to reach South Carolina were the Spanish, in the early 1500s. Later in the 1500s French Protestants settled there. English settlement began in the later 1600s. Englishmen of wealth from the West Indies developed rice and indigo production, and the coastal lowlands produced sea-island cotton. The wealth derived by the planters from these crops helped to build the lovely old homes of Charleston, one of the most charming of the historic cities of the United States.

West of the port city of Charleston is a long stretch of land that rises gradually to the Piedmont Plateau. The Plateau, in turn, rises to the Blue Ridge Mountains in the western part of the state. This expanse of land encompasses farms and timberlands, and industrial sites. Columbia, the capital of South Carolina, and Spartanburg are the state's major industrial centers. Aiken is renowned for its fine golf courses and for its polo. South Carolina's shore has delightful resorts, excellent beaches, and good saltwater fishing.

Tennessee

The first European to reach Tennessee may well have been a Spaniard, Hernando de Soto, in the 1540s. In the 1670s two Frenchmen, Louis Jolliet and Jacques Marquette, explored the Mississippi River as far south as Arkansas. But permanent European settlement came in the 1700s, and the region was explored by Daniel Boone.

Tennessee was an important battleground of the Civil War, with Tennesseans serving in the armies of both the Union and the Confederacy. The great battles of Shiloh, Chattanooga, and bloody Lookout Mountain and Missionary Ridge were all fought on Tennessee soil.

The face of the state was radically changed in the 1930s, when the Tennessee Valley Authority (TVA) brought the brawling flood waters of the Tennessee and Cumberland rivers under control. Electricity was brought to areas throughout the state, and cheap power fostered economic growth. Today Tennessee is the home of the Oak Ridge center of the U.S. Atomic Energy Commission.

Nashville, the capital of the state, is a delightful old city surrounded by rich farmland. It is known as the home of "country" music, and it is one of the major entertainment centers of the United States. It is also an important commercial and financial center. Memphis, a major inland port and cotton market, is famous also as an early center of jazz. Knoxville, in the foothills of the Smoky Mountains, is the commercial and industrial center of eastern Tennessee. The Great Smoky Mountains National Park is one of the most beautiful and popular forest reserves of the eastern United States.

Georgia

"The Empire State of the South," the land of cotton and red clay, of coastal lowlands and swamp, Georgia epitomizes the "Deep South." Although the first Europeans to reach Georgia were Spanish, permanent settlement began in the 1730s at Savannah under Sir James Oglethorpe. Oglethorpe built a fort on St. Simon Island to protect the English settlement from the Spanish in Florida to the south, and the red-brick ruins of the fort, shaded by huge old oaks, are truly memorable.

The land rises from coastal lowlands — the Marshes of Glynn and the Okefenokee Swamp — to the Piedmont Plateau. Mountains dominate the far north. Georgia's sea islands once produced a fine long-staple cotton, but today they are the home of fine resorts. The beautiful old port city of Savannah continues to handle considerable traffic in agricultural goods. Macon, in the heart of the state's famous peach-orchard region, is a picturesque city. It was the home of the poet Sidney Lanier, and Macon's Wesleyan College is the oldest women's college in the country. Augusta, on the Savannah River, is the site of the famous annual Masters Golf Tournament. It is also a producer of textiles and clay products.

Atlanta, burned to the ground in the Civil War, today is a handsome, booming metropolis, the major financial and industrial center of the Southeast. The city has both drive and elegance, and it is surrounded by beautiful residential suburbs. Nearby Stone Mountain, an enormous granite dome with the carved likenesses of Confederate President Jefferson Davis and generals Stonewall Jackson and Robert E. Lee, is set amid a park. It is one of the most charming recreational spots of the region.

Florida

Almost a century before the English founded their first settlement at Jamestown in 1607, Spanish explorers had reached Florida. And in 1565 the Spanish founded St. Augustine, the oldest permanent European settlement on the North American mainland.

The red clay foothills of the Appalachians descend all the way down to Tallahassee, Florida's capital, an old, charming city, and the only Southern capital the North did not capture during the Civil War. At the other end of Florida lies Key West, the southernmost city of the United States. A lovely old town, it is surrounded by emerald-green waters.

Although Florida contains the country's oldest city, most of the state is young. Cape Kennedy, a symbol of the space age, is the launching site of space vehicles. Walt Disney World is transforming the rolling, citrus-clad hills around Orlando, and attracting tens of thousands of tourists every week, Miami, on Biscayne Bay, entertains millions of visitors with its horse races and dog races and its night clubs, and with jai-alai from Spain's Basque country and theatrical killer whales from the North Pacific in the Seaquarium. Miami is also home to hundreds of thousands of Cuban refugees. Miami Beach, across the bay, became a city only in 1915 and is today the biggest winter resort in the U.S.A.

The woodlands of northern Florida are a rich source of pulpwood. The orange groves of central Florida produce much of the country's orange crop. And the vegetable fields of the southern part of the state produce much of the fresh vegetables — tomatoes, beans, and sweet corn — that colder parts of the country eat in winter.

Alabama

Present-day Alabama was explored by Hernando de Soto in the 1500s, but the first permanent settlement was made by the French in the early 1700s at Mobile. It became English in the 1760s.

Products of the earth have shaped Alabama — cotton, coal, and iron. Before the Civil War, Alabama cotton fed the hungry mills of New England. But the war left the economy of the state in ruins. By the turn of the century, however, the coal and iron around Birmingham made that city a great industrial center. Agriculture has been diversified, and today the principal crop of the old "Cotton State" is corn. The hilly northern part of the state has deposits of coal and marble, and it draws power from the great TVA system.

Huntsville, in northern Alabama, is the site of the George C. Marshall Space Flight Center, the developer of the Saturn rocket. Mobile continues to be a gracious city. Its excellent deep-water port on Mobile Bay has made it a major port of the United States and a leading shipbuilding center. Mobile is also the home port of a large commercial fishing fleet that brings in oysters and fish from the Gulf of Mexico. Jefferson Davis was sworn in as president of the Confederacy on the steps of the state capitol in Montgomery. Still a dignified city, Montgomery has become a manufacturing center.

Alabama has many recreational facilities. The state's white beaches on the Gulf of Mexico draw vacationers southward. The forests of the Appalachian highlands are popular for camping and fishing. Alabama is one of the finest quail-hunting states in the country, and the forests also contain other game, including deer and turkey.

Mississippi

Mississippi was originally part of French Louisiana, and the first permanent European settlement was made at Biloxi in 1699 by Pierre Lemoyne, Sieur d'Iberville.

A fine way to become acquainted with Mississippi is to follow the old Natchez Trace along the Mississippi River. In the early 1800s, the Natchez Trace was a pioneer roadway. Today it is the Natchez Trace Parkway.

No part of the South can boast more beautiful ante-bellum homes than Mississippi. They were built with the wealth derived from the fine cotton grown in the fertile black soil of the delta region. Many of the state's elegant mansions are on the high bluffs near Natchez, a romantic Mississippi River port that had its golden age in the first half of the 1800s. Many of the old homes are open to the public during an annual spring fete, in March.

Jackson, the capital and largest city of Mississippi, once a trading post, is an industrial and educational center. It is also the home of Eudora Welty, one of the South's major writers, who captured the life of rural Mississippi in her stories. But perhaps no other section of the state has achieved the renown of Yoknapatawpha County, novelist William Faulkner's mythical setting for his saga of the Snopes clan.

Louisiana

There is a magic about Louisiana compounded of visions of lacy iron grillwork, jazz, Creole cooking, and old mansions in the bayou country. It is a world with a style of its own, a style to which France, Spain, and Africa have contributed mightily. Claimed by the French in the 1680s, later in Spanish hands, and then again French, Louisiana was purchased by the United States in 1803.

Louisiana is not only rich in romance; it is a state rich in natural resources. Agriculture continues to play an important role in the state's economic life, and Louisiana is an important producer of cotton, rice, cane sugar, and pecans. The state also produces about a million barrels of oil a day, and there are hundreds of oil and gas fields in southern and northern Louisiana. Sulphur is also a valuable product, and Louisiana is a major producer of pulpwood. Fishing in the Gulf of Mexico and in the delta is excellent.

New Orleans, a major U.S. port at the mouth of the Mississippi River, is well known for its charming French Quarter, its restaurants, and its music. Perhaps it is best known, however for its Mardi Gras, a true festival of revelry. Baton Rouge, the state's beautiful old capital, is an industrial center as well as the focal point of state politics. Shreveport, in the north, is a lively city in a region rich in cotton, oil, and natural gas.

Texas

In the 1820s, generous Mexican land grants drew thousands of U.S. citizens to Mexico's northern province of Texas. In 1836 the U.S. settlers officially declared their independence of Mexico and established the republic of Texas, which lasted for a decade, until Texas joined the Union in 1846.

After the Civil War, veterans of the defeated Confederate armies turned to rounding up wild longhorn cattle and driving them up the Chisholm Trail to the cattle market in Abilene, Kansas. These men became the models for the popular figure of Western lore, the cowboy. The great cattle drives were ended as fences were built and as railroads penetrated the southwest. A new wave of migration to Texas came from agriculturally depressed areas of the Deep South in the 1870s and 1880s.

Texas is still a top producer of cattle, as well as of wheat and cotton, but today the state is best known for its oil. The first shallow well was brought in in 1894 and the first gusher on the Gulf Coast prairie in 1901. Oil was struck in West Texas in 1923, and in 1930 the big East Texas field was tapped. The discovery and exploitation of these vast deposits of oil wrought a revolution in the lives of the people of Texas.

Fabulous accumulations of wealth from oil spurred the growth of Texas cities. Houston, 50 miles from the Gulf of Mexico, is a major port of the United States, due to the Houston Ship Channel. It is the undisputed oil capital of the world, and most of the world's oil-drilling equipment is produced there. Houston is also the home of the Manned Spacecraft Center, which focuses the eyes of the world on Houston during voyages to the moon.

Oil also fueled the growth of Dallas and Fort Worth, skyscraper cities of the plain. Although it too has added skyscrapers, San Antonio, cradle of Texas liberty, still retains much of its eighteenth century Spanish flavor.

Oklahoma

In the first half of the 1800s, Oklahoma was Indian Territory, and Cherokees, Creeks, Chickasaws, Choctaws, and Seminoles were moved to Oklahoma where they were given title to lands. Comanches, Kiowas, and Apaches were also rounded up and moved to reservations in the territory. But in the late 1800s, Congress bought back the Indian lands and in 1889 Oklahoma was opened to settlers. In the first land rush, towns were born in a day. Nonetheless, members of more than 60 Indian tribes still live in Oklahoma.

Oklahoma is a fascinating state of mesas, rolling plains, and alabaster caverns. The plains slope upward to the wooded hills of the Ozarks in the northeast and to the Ouachita Mountains in the southeast. Much of the plain is given over to diversified agriculture, including cattle raising. Oklahoma is also a major producer of oil and natural gas, and there are deposits of lead, coal, and zinc.

Oklahoma City, the state capital, is a financial and commercial center. Its capitol building stands on a large oilfield and is ringed with oil derricks.

THE SOUTH

Arkansas

Acquired by the United States in 1803 as part of the Louisiana Purchase, Arkansas joined the Union in 1836. The area had been settled largely by Southerners, and Arkansas fought with the Confederacy in the Civil War.

Handsome forests cover about two thirds of the state, and timber is an important element in its economic life. Bauxite, from which aluminum is produced, is also important. The part of the state that lies in the Mississippi Valley is rich farmland, with cotton, rice, and soybeans major crops. Poultry and cattle raising are thriving industries. Although Arkansas is primarily an agricultural state, manufacturing has been growing.

Little Rock, capital of the state, has been called the City of Roses. It is perched on a rocky bluff above the Arkansas River, and it is an industrial, financial, and transportation center. The Ouachita National Forest and the Ozark National Forest, in the western part of the state, with their fine fishing, camping, and hunting grounds are favorite retreats of lovers of the woodlands. Hot Springs, midst a National Park of the same name, is a noted spa with 47 hot mineral springs not far from Little Rock.

Puerto Rico

Although not part of the U.S. South, Puerto Rico is certainly geographically southern. This "Free and Associated State" of the United States is Spanish in its cultural heritage and language. With its near-perfect climate, magnificent beaches, and flower-filled mountain forests, Puerto Rico was reached by Columbus in 1493. Juan Ponce de León began the exploration of the island in 1508, and Spanish settlement followed. Puerto Rico became a U.S. territory in 1899, after the Spanish-American War. The island, 3435 square miles in area, remained poor despite its beauty, however.

In 1917 the people of Puerto Rico were granted U.S. citizenship, and in 1948 Puerto Ricans chose their first popularly-elected governor, Luis Muñoz Marin. The Commonwealth of Puerto Rico was proclaimed in 1952, and an ambitious economic development program, Operation Bootstrap, was launched. Under this self-help program, industry increased and Puerto Rico became a major tourist center for people from the mainland.

San Juan, Puerto Rico's capital, is a study in contrasts. The Old City, with its massive fortresses and narrow streets dating back to the 1500s, has retained much of its Spanish colonial atmosphere. The newer sections of the city contain modern apartment houses, luxury hotels, and wide boulevards. The island's excellent roads lead from San Juan to the cities of Ponce and Mayaguez, to Luquillo Beach and to El Yunque, the fabled tropical rain forest.

The U.S. Virgin Islands

Also far to the south geographically are the Virgin Islands, just east of Puerto Rico. The islands were once the home of the fierce Carib Indians, who successfully fought off the Spanish and Dutch. Denmark took possession of part of the islands in the 1600s, however, and successfully colonized them. The three larger islands — St. Thomas, St. Croix, and St. John — were purchased by the United States during World War I; the remaining islands are British. Today the U.S. islands form an unincorporated territory under the jurisdiction of the Department of the Interior. The residents are citizens of the United States and elect their own local government officials.

The Virgin Islands are popular with tourists, who flock principally to St. Thomas. Charlotte Amalie, the capital, is a delightful eighteenth-century town with an excellent deep-water harbor. Its great free-port shopping center is a mecca to tourists seeking bargains.

St. Croix, largest of the U.S. islands, is an agricultural and industrial land. Christiansted, its small, red-roofed capital, was once capital of all the Danish islands. St. John, the third of the major islands, is a quiet island with green mountains, cool streams, forest tracts, and beaches. On St. John is Virgin Island National Park, created by a gift of 5,000 acres of land to the United States by Lawrence Rockefeller.

THE SOUTH
Description of the following pictures

page 97 VIRGINIA

MOUNT VERNON, VIRGINIA

A short drive from Washington is Mount Vernon, George Washington's home overlooking the Potomac River. It is an excellent example of late eighteenth century architecture. Inheriting a modest-sized house, Washington more than doubled its size in the years between 1745 and 1799. To support the elegant mansion, he created an extensive "village" of service buildings, most of which have survived. The main house and nearly a dozen of the surviving service buildings offer the visitor a glimpse into the homelife of an eighteenth-century American aristocrat. At the foot of the vineyard enclosure is George Washington's tomb.

GOVERNOR'S PALACE

Home and office for royal governors when Virginia was under the British Crown, this magnificent building was also "home" to Patrick Henry and Thomas Jefferson during their tenures as governors of the Commonwealth of Virginia. The gardens have trim hedges thickly set in eighteenth century style, and precise geometrical walkways lead through no fewer than ten separate gardens. Plants and fruit trees flower in planned profusion throughout each season.

page 98 WASHINGTON, D.C.

THE SUPREME COURT

Completed only in the 1930s, the Supreme Court building looks like a Grecian temple. Built of white marble and with vast Corinthian columns, the building reflects the power and prestige of the nation's highest tribunal and the majesty of the law.

page 99 WASHINGTON, D.C.

THE U.S. CAPITOL

The Capitol is one of the most inspiring buildings in the United States. The magnificent dome is topped by Thomas Crawford's statue of Freedom. The hilltop site selected by Pierre Charles L'Enfant, who planned the capital in the 1790s, makes the Capitol dome visible for miles. Housing the legislative branch of the federal government, the Capitol, in a sense, is a self-contained community. It has its own prayer room, post offices, underground railway system, restaurants, police force, and even barbershops. Millions of people visit the Capitol each year.

THE WHITE HOUSE

Next to the Capitol, the most popular tourist site in Washington, D.C., is the White House, the official residence of the president and his family. The cornerstone of this beautiful mansion was laid in 1792 and, despite almost continuous renovation, the White House has preserved the essentials of its beginnings. It contains some of the finest representations of U.S. furnishings. The splendid grounds, with their well-manicured lawns, contain some 80 varieties of trees, including birches, red maples, tulip trees, and bald cypresses. Two trees, with trunks seven feet in diameter, are believed to be more than 150 years old.

page 100   VIRGINIA
OAK HILL, LEESBURG, VIRGINIA
Nine miles south of Leesburg stands Oak Hill, the home of James Monroe, fifth president of the United States. Thomas Jefferson designed the house and James Hoban, who designed the White House, supervised its construction. Congress presented President Monroe oaks from every state then in the Union, and they were planted there. Oak Hill is today one of the best known of the outstanding old homes of Virginia.

BERKELEY PLANTATION, JAMES RIVER, VIRGINIA
Known as the Berkeley Hundred, these acres were part of a grant awarded by England's King James I in 1619. There, in accordance with the Berkeley Company's instructions, "the day of our ships' arrival . . . shall be

yearly and perpetually kept as a day of Thanksgiving," and on December 4, 1619, the first Thanksgiving Day was celebrated. The lovely old mansion was built in 1726 by Benjamin Harrison and was host to George Washington. It was the ancestral home of two presidents, William Henry Harrison and Benjamin Harrison, and during the Civil War General Daniel Butterfield composed "Taps" there.

page 101   NORTH CAROLINA
RHODODENDRON ON ROAN MOUNTAIN, NORTH CAROLINA
The western mountains of North Carolina are covered with flowering rhododendron each June. The largest natural rhododendron garden is near Bakersville, on Roan Mountain, in Pisgah National Forest.

page 102   SOUTH CAROLINA
ST. MICHAEL'S CHURCH, CHARLESTON, SOUTH CAROLINA
One of the oldest churches in Charleston, built in the 1750s, St. Michael's is located on the grounds of a still earlier church, St. Philip's, which was built in the 1680s. St. Michael's is designed on the model of London's St. Martins-in-the-Fields. Its steeple-crowned tower rises more than 180 feet above the ground and is a landmark in Charleston, one

95

of the oldest U.S. cities. Charleston, an early colonial port with an excellent harbor, has preserved much of the atmosphere of the eighteenth century, and it is filled with beautiful old houses.

THE STATE HOUSE, COLUMBIA, SOUTH CAROLINA

Construction of the South Carolina capitol began just before the Civil War, which prevented its completion. Union General William T. Sherman spared the building, which he recognized as a work of art, but some shells struck the walls of the gray granite Italian Renaissance Style structure. The shell marks are covered by bronze stars.

page 102   NORTH CAROLINA
LATHAM GARDEN, NEW BERN, NORTH CAROLINA

Latham Garden is part of Tryon Palace, once the colonial capitol of North Carolina and the home of William Tryon, a royal governor. When it was built in 1770, the mansion and gardens were described as the most beautiful in colonial America. The buildings and gardens have been restored to their original grandeur, and the gardens are still landscaped in the manner of eighteenth century English gardens. New Bern, settled in 1710 by German and Swiss colonists, was the meeting place of the colonial assembly and the seat of royal governors of North Carolina.

page 103   GEORGIA
PEACHTREE CENTER, ATLANTA, GEORGIA

Atlanta, capital of Georgia, is a symbol of the New South. Burned to the ground during the Civil War, Atlanta emerged a century later as the leading economic center of the Southeastern United States. A fine example of its outstanding modern architecture is the Peachtree Center, on the city's well-known Peachtree Street.

page 104   FLORIDA
WALT DISNEY WORLD, FLORIDA

Located in central Florida near Orlando, Walt Disney World is one of the outstanding tourist attractions of the United States. Many thousands of visitors arrive there every day from all parts of the world. It is a vacation kingdom with fine hotels; golf courses; facilities for such water sports as sailing, skiing, and boating; tennis courts; and camp sites. The attractions are spread among six major areas: Adventureland, Frontierland, Fantasyland, Liberty Square, Main Street U.S.A., and Tomorrowland. Florida's Walt Disney World is a family-oriented resort, a place for a family to stay for a week or two. The hotels, recreation, and entertainment facilities are linked by a unique transportation network that includes monorail, steam boats, and surface vehicles. There is also a 12,000-car parking area.

(Continued on page 117)

MOUNT VERNON

VIRGINIA

GOVERNORS PALACE, WILLIAMSBURG

THE SUPREME COURT

WASHINGTON, D.C.

THE U.S. CAPITOL

THE WHITE HOUSE

OAK HILL, LEESBURG

VIRGINIA

BERKELEY PLANTATION
JAMES RIVER

→

RHODODENDRON
ON ROAN MOUNTAIN
NORTH CAROLINA

ST. MICHAELS CHURCH, CHARLESTON,
SOUTH CAROLINA

STATE HOUSE, COLUMBIA, SOUTH CAROLINA

LATHAM GARDEN,
NEW BERN,
NORTH CAROLINA

102

PEACHTREE CENTER, ATLANTA, GEORGIA

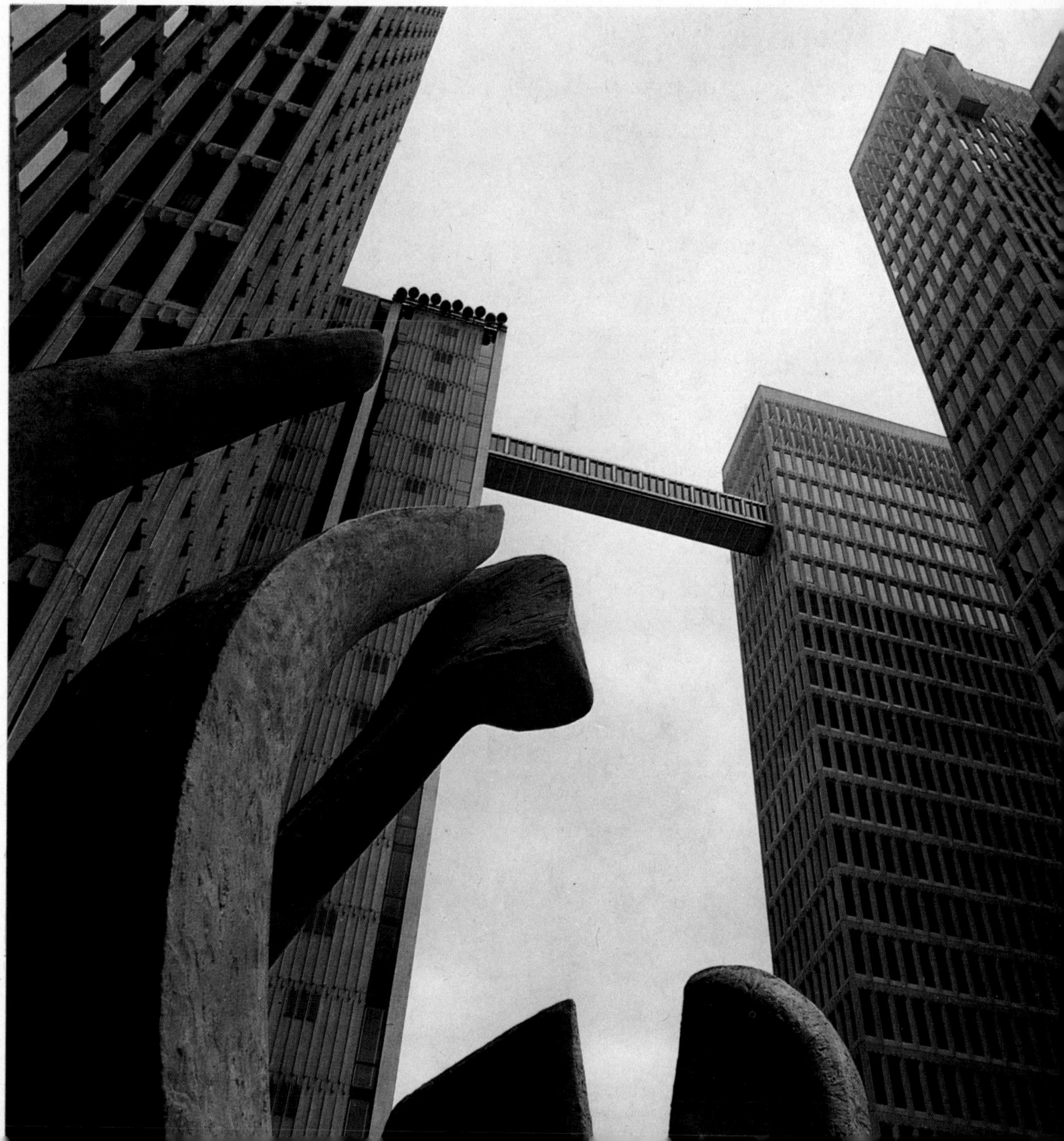

WALT DISNEY WORLD

SEMINOLE INDIANS, EVERGLADES

FLORIDA

MIAMI BEACH

SKYLINE AND
YACHT HARBOR,
MIAMI

FLORIDA

FLORIDA
CITRUS HARVEST

CASTILLO DE SAN MARCOS
OLDEST FORT IN U.S.A.
1672-1756

**ST. AUGUSTINE,
FLORIDA
OLDEST TOWN
IN THE U.S.A.
1565**

THE R.C. CATHEDRAL
1793

106

CHRISTIANSTED
ST. CROIX

CANEEL BAY
ST. JOHN

**U.S. VIRGIN
ISLANDS**

HARBOR
OF ST. THOMAS

ANCIENT AND MODERN
SAN JUAN

PUERTO RICO

LUQUILLO BEACH

NEW ORLEANS, LOUISIANA

BELLINGRATH GARDENS
MOBILE, ALABAMA

TEXAS

SKYLINE, DALLAS

THE ALAMO, SAN ANTONIO

HOUSTON

NASA MANNED SPACE CENTER, CLEAR LAKE

SANTA ELENA CANYON
BIG BEND NATIONAL PARK
TEXAS

OKLAHOMA INDIANS

112

LITTLE ROCK

ARKANSAS

HOT SPRINGS NATIONAL PARK

HORSE FARM

MAMMOTH CAVE
NATIONAL PARK

KENTUCKY

TOBACCO FIELD

GRAVE OF DANIEL BOONE
FRANKFORT

ABRAHAM LINCOLN
MEMORIAL, HODGENVILLE

KENTUCKY

CHURCHILL
DOWNS,
LOUISVILLE

NASHVILLE

TENNESSEE

MEMPHIS

116

Description of foregoing pictures
Continued from page 96

Continued from page 96

page 104   FLORIDA

SEMINOLE INDIANS, EVERGLADES

Seminole means "people of distant lives," and the Florida Indians living in south Florida today are descended from tribes that came from far away, from Georgia's Creek Indians, the Muscogees, and from the Miccosukee tribe of north Florida. A proud and handsome people, the Seminoles in Florida today represent only a part of those who fought the fierce Seminole Indian Wars in the early nineteenth century. They still stick to their traditional way of life, wear their old costumes deep in the cypress forests and swamps of the Everglades, live in their palmetto-thatched chickees in small villages.

MIAMI BEACH

Florida's greatest playground, Miami Beach, offers its millions of visitors accommodations in hundreds of luxury hotels and motels that rise beside the soft sands of its beaches. The photograph shows part of Miami Beach's hotel row between the ocean front and Indian Creek. Just to the left can be seen something of the residential section — homes with large, tropical gardens and golf courses.

page 105   FLORIDA

SKYLINE AND YACHT HARBOR OF MIAMI

Today Miami is Florida's most populous city, with more than 1,400,000 people in its metropolitan area. The cosmopolitan city is a gateway to the Caribbean, Central and South America, and to Europe. Its harbor, home port of many luxurious cruise ships is one of the busiest in the United States, its "Miamarina" one of the most modern and elegant yacht harbors in Florida.

CITRUS HARVEST, FLORIDA

Florida is covered with citrus groves, particularly in the center and south, and the state is the major citrus producer of the United States. This photo, taken at the Flamingo Groves near Fort Lauderdale, shows orange trees to the left and grapefruit trees to the right.

page 106   FLORIDA

CASTILLO DE SAN MARCOS, ST. AUGUSTINE

This is the oldest standing fort in the United States. Construction of this moated fortress was begun in 1672 and completed in 1756.

117

Erected with the help of Indian hostages, Negro slaves, soldiers and inhabitants of the city, this stronghold has outer walls twelve feet thick tapering to seven feet at the top, all constructed of coquina blocks quarried on nearby Anastasia Island.

R. C. CATHEDRAL, ST. AUGUSTINE, FLORIDA

The oldest permanent European settlement in the United States, St. Augustine was established in 1565 by Pedro Menéndez de Avilés. The area had been claimed for Spain in 1513 by Juan Ponce de León. The cathedral, begun in 1793, lies in the heart of the old city. The park shown in the photo was originally the scene of religious celebrations and was used as a military parade ground.

page 107 U.S. VIRGIN ISLANDS
CHRISTIANSTED, ST. CROIX

This well-preserved Danish port was for many years capital of the Danish Virgin Islands. With its romantic streets and interesting historical buildings painted in pastel colors, it is one of the highlights of every Caribbean visit.

CANEEL BAY, ST. JOHN

The Virgin Islands are filled with secluded beaches like the one pictured here. The sands are powder soft, the waters translucent blue or green, marvelous for skin-diving and underwater exploration. At Caneel Bay on the quiet island of St. John is one of the outstanding resorts, Caneel Bay Plantation, built with all modern conveniences into the ruins of an ancient Danish plantation.

HARBOR OF ST. THOMAS

One of the great views of St. Thomas: As we look down from the terrace of Bluebeard's Castle, the harbor of St. Thomas and the city of Charlotte Amalie surround us with a unique setting. To the right is Charlotte Amalie; in the background French Town and Water Island. In front is a Royal Poinciana tree in full bloom, a glory of the Caribbean.

page 108 PUERTO RICO
ANCIENT AND MODERN SAN JUAN

This view from the Caribe Hilton Hotel to the modern Condado section of San Juan shows, in the foreground, the historic Fort San Jerónimo, one of three small forts built to protect the landward end of San Juan Island. It played an important role during the English attacks by Drake (1595) and Abercromby (1797). When Admiral Drake attacked San Juan, attracted by the rumor that a great Mexican treasure fleet had arrived, a chance cannon shot from San Jerónimo struck the Admiral's dinner table, killing three captains who were dining with him. This so enraged Drake that he set fire to a Spanish ship in the harbor. The blaze illuminated his own fleet so brightly that the guns of El Morro were successful in destroying almost half of the Admiral's ships. In the background some of the fine hotels of San Juan are visible: San Jerónimo, La Concha, Puerto Rico Sheraton and Flamboyan.

LUQUILLO BEACH

A few miles east of San Juan is the magnificent, popular beach, Luquillo. It ranks among the most beautiful beaches in the world: crescent-shaped, covered with fine white sand, surrounded by a forest of coconut palms. The waters are calm, clear, blue-green in color. It is well-kept by the Puerto Rican government.

page 109   THE SOUTH

NEW ORLEANS, LOUISIANA

A view from the third floor of Le Prêtre Mansion, at the corner of Dauphine and Orleans streets, provides a beautiful contrast of old and new New Orleans. The modern office buildings of downtown, with the Hibernia Tower in the middle, are framed by the antique cast-iron lacework of the balcony.

BELLINGRATH GARDENS, MOBILE, ALABAMA

Mobile, an important port on the Gulf of Mexico, is a wealthy city with beautiful homes, old and new, and magnificent gardens. The best known of Mobile's gardens is Bellingrath, about 20 miles north of the city proper. The 65-acre garden, which blooms the year round, is famous for its azaleas and camelias.

page 110   TEXAS

SKYLINE DALLAS

Founded in 1841 as a trading post, Dallas began to grow rapidly when the railroad reached the sleepy settlement. By 1886 it was a busy transportation center, with six railroads carrying cattle, cotton, wheat, and wool. Early in the 1900s, a city planning league was created to control the growth of the city. The league developed into a city department of urban development, and today Dallas' city planning is as impressive as its skyline. In addition to great business establishments, Dallas has rich cultural facilities. The city is famous for its theater and music, and for its sports events and state fair.

THE ALAMO, SAN ANTONIO

The Mission San Antonio de Valero, in downtown San Antonio, was established in 1718 by Franciscan fathers as a center for the conversion of the Indians. By 1744 the church and fortifications, the Alamo, were built. The Alamo became a shrine during the Texas struggle for independence from Mexico when a small group of Texans held the fort against a large Mexican army for two weeks in 1836.

page 111   TEXAS

HOUSTON

The largest and one of the most modern cities of the Southwest, Houston is a leading industrial and commercial center. It is also a major port. The city is named for Sam Houston, hero of the battle of San Jacinto, which won Texas its independence from Mexico.

NASA MANNED SPACE CENTER, CLEAR LAKE, TEXAS

About 20 miles southeast of Houston is the NASA Manned Space Center. Development of the center brought many related industries to the area and contributed greatly to Houston's economic growth.

page 112

SANTA ELENA CANYON, BIG BEND NATIONAL PARK, TEXAS

Spectacular wild desert and mountain scenery is found in Big Bend National Park in southwestern Texas, on the border with Mexico. The park covers an area of more than 700,000 acres within a large bend of the Rio Grande, which flows through three big gorges, one of which is Santa Elena Canyon. The colorful cliffs are more than 1500 feet high.

OKLAHOMA INDIANS

A considerable part of Oklahoma was set aside in the early 1800s as Indian territory, and five tribes from the southern states were brought there by military force. Today more than 60 Indian tribes live in Oklahoma. This photo was taken at Gallup, New Mexico, where Indians from Oklahoma and several other states held annual meetings in mid-August.

page 113   ARKANSAS

LITTLE ROCK, ARKANSAS

The capital of Arkansas, Little Rock is situated on the Arkansas River. The State Capitol dominates the modern, high-rising city. In MacArthur Park is the Arkansas Arts Center, with galleries displaying collections of paintings, sculpture, and ceramics, and a theater.

HOT SPRINGS NATIONAL PARK, ARKANSAS

Hot Springs, Arkansas, is one of the outstanding spas of the United States. Known to the Indians long before Columbus reached the New World, it was called Tah-ne-co, the valley of the vapors. Indians of many tribes came to bathe in the waters, which they held sacred. In 1804 President Thomas Jefferson sent scientists to investigate the thermal waters. In 1832 President Andrew Jackson signed the law that established Hot Springs as a U.S. government reservation, to be preserved for all time as a national resource. Today it is a national park of more than 1000 acres. Beautiful slopes surround the attractive resort town of Hot Springs.

page 114   KENTUCKY
MAMMOTH CAVE NATIONAL PARK
Established as a national park in 1938, the caves were once privately owned. The photo shows Frozen Niagara, discovered in 1923, one of the most beautiful formations to be seen in the world-famous caves, which lie in southern Kentucky, near Bowling Green.

HORSE FARM, LEXINGTON
One of Kentucky's greatest attractions is its horse farms, with their white fences and handsome barns. There are more than 200 horse farms in the state, and they breed and raise some of the finest horses to be found in the United States.

TOBACCO FIELD
One of Kentucky's major crops, tobacco was grown there by the Indians long before European settlers arrived. Commercial tobacco growing began in the late 1700s, and a number of varieties have been developed. The light, air-cured Burley is the leading variety.

page 115   KENTUCKY
GRAVE OF DANIEL BOONE, FRANKFORT
Born in Pennsylvania in 1734, Daniel Boone helped open Kentucky to settlement. He first visited the area in 1767. He returned in 1769 and spent two years exploring the region. In 1775 he brought his family and a party of settlers, founding what is now Boonesboro. He died in 1820 and his grave is in Frankfort, Kentucky's capital.

ABRAHAM LINCOLN MEMORIAL, HODGENVILLE
The small log cabin in which Abraham Lincoln was born in 1809 is enclosed by a granite memorial. Above the entrance to the memorial, which is on Sinking Spring Farm near Hodgenville, Kentucky, are Lincoln's words: "With malice toward none, with charity for all."

CHURCHILL DOWNS, LOUISVILLE
Horse racing in Louisville goes back to the early days of the city, which was laid out in 1779, and the Kentucky Derby has been run every year beginning in 1875. Derby Day, the first Saturday of May, draws the attention of the race-loving public throughout the nation. Preceding the race are ten days of festivities.

PHOTO DESCRIPTIONS (SOUTH)

page 116

TENNESSEE

NASHVILLE

Capital of Tennessee, Nashville is rapidly becoming a modern city with high-rise buildings and wide, elegant streets. The handsome State Capitol, completed in 1809, overlooks the city, founded in 1779 on the west bank of the Cumberland River.

MEMPHIS

One of the most progressive cities of the South, Memphis was once a brawling boom town served by Mississippi River steamboats. The city was founded in 1819 on a site chosen because of the high bluffs and the excellent river landing. Andrew Jackson played an important role in the early development of the town, which grew rapidly as German and Scottish settlers arrived from central Tennessee. Today Memphis is one of the largest cotton markets of the world, an educational and medical center of the South, and the largest city of Tennessee.

THE NORTH CENTRAL STATES

OHIO

INDIANA

ILLINOIS

MICHIGAN

WISCONSIN

MINNESOTA

NORTH DAKOTA

SOUTH DAKOTA

NEBRASKA

IOWA

KANSAS

MISSOURI

THE NORTH CENTRAL STATES

Ohio, Indiana, Illinois, Michigan, Wisconsin, Minnesota, North Dakota, South Dakota, Nebraska, Iowa, Kansas, Missouri

The region between the Appalachians and the Rockies, the area occupied by the North Central States, has been called the heartland of the United States. There are found the largest farms and the biggest industrial complexes. A seemingly endless flow of corn and soybeans, wheat and rye, potatoes and dairy products, beef and pork, steel and iron, and machinery and automobiles pours forth. From this land inhabited by vigorous descendants of immigrants from all parts of Europe and from Africa have come such men as Henry Ford, Elbert Gary, and John D. Rockefeller.

In the decades since World War II, the region has seen a rapid economic expansion. Farms have become larger in size and agriculture has become more and more a commercial activity. Industrial plants have pushed into old farm communities and colleges and universities, technical schools and research institutes have been established and expanded to meet the needs of modern industrial society in rapid change.

This inland world, although thousands of miles from the oceans, has many seaports. The water complex of the Great Lakes is linked to the Atlantic Ocean through the St. Lawrence Seaway, allowing ocean-going vessels to dock more than 2000 miles from East Coast ports. Access to the Gulf of Mexico is provided by the great rivers of the region — the Ohio, the Mississippi, and the Missouri. But the rivers of the area have been responsible for disastrous floods and the government has pursued vast programs to tame them with networks of dams and levees.

Ohio

The men who set out to settle the Ohio Valley after the American Revolution met Miami Indians intent on preserving their homeland. The land the settlers finally claimed in 1794 had seen much bloodshed. After the adoption of the Northwest Ordinance in 1787, the peopling of Ohio, the central state of the old Northwest Territory, made rapid progress. New Englanders, Pennsylvanians, Virginians, and many others poured into this new part of the country. After the end of the Civil War, in the second half of the 1800s, these earlier immigrants were joined by others from Germany and northern Europe. Still later, immigrants from southern and eastern Europe began to arrive; and in still more recent times the poor of the South, both black and white, moved into the area.

Extensive coal deposits and access to the Great Lakes through Lake Erie ports, and its Ohio River ports, helped make Ohio a great industrial state. But even today more than half its land is still farmed, with corn, wheat, and soybeans among the major cash crops. The state's vigorous industrial cities include Akron, Canton, Columbus, Dayton, and Youngstown. The first center of industry was the Ohio River port of Cincinnati. Cleveland, on Lake Erie, also became a major industrial center in the 1800s, and it was there that John D. Rockefeller began building a great industrial and financial empire.

Cleveland, Ohio's largest city, has become a major cultural center. Its universities, its art museum, and its symphony orchestra have all won world renown. Cincinnati has also become a famous center of intellectual activity. The shores of Lake Erie, although threatened by pollution, remain a summer vacationland. And winter skiing is increasingly popular in the Appalachians.

Indiana

The first European settlement in what is now Indiana was made by the French at Vincennes in about 1700. The first U.S. settlement was established in the 1780s. For a decade after the American Revolution, the area was the scene of bloody warfare between Indians and settlers, but once peace prevailed settlers began to arrive in increasing numbers.

The center of the state is a level, fertile plain, and Indiana's farms are important producers of grain, fruit, tobacco, hogs, and dairy cattle. Lake Michigan in the north and the Ohio River in the south provide access to raw materials and to markets, and Indiana's industry is well developed. The Calumet region in the north, which includes Gary, Hammond, and East Chicago, is an important industrial center. Evansville, Fort Wayne, Muncie, Terre Haute, and South Bend are all leading manufacturing cities.

Indianapolis, the state capital, lies in the central part of the state and is surrounded by large coal fields and rich fields of corn and wheat. It is the home of the Indianapolis Speedway, which draws huge crowds to the annual 500-mile Memorial Day auto race.

The dunes and beaches along Lake Michigan in the north and the lovely woodlands of the Hoosier National Forest in the south are popular vacation and recreation spots.

Illinois

The area of present-day Illinois was explored by the French in the 1600s, and the state is liberally sprinkled with French names — Des Plaines, Joliet, La Salle.

In the years preceding the Civil War, slavery became a major issue in Illinois, which had joined the Union in 1818. The issue was reflected in a historic series of debates between two of the state's most illustrious political figures — Abraham Lincoln and Stephen A. Douglas. Illinois voters chose Douglas to represent them in the Senate of the United States, and the nation later elected Lincoln to the presidency.

Today Illinois is a land of contrasts. Vast agricultural tracts border coal and gas fields and tremendous industrial complexes. The leisurely air of southern Illinois farming communities stands apart from the ever-changing, fast-paced atmosphere of urban, industrial northern Illinois.

The birthplace of the skyscraper, Chicago lies on the shores of Lake Michigan. This truly "Windy City," with its gleaming new buildings, its vitality, and its world-famous universities and museums is a key economic center of the United States as well as of the North Central States. Chicago is a major port, through the St. Lawrence Seaway, and a major distribution point. The iron and coal of the Lake Superior region is brought to Chicago to feed its vast manufacturing complex. And Chicago's commodity markets and financial institutions serve large parts of the country.

Springfield, the capital of Illinois, lies in the heart of one of the richest agricultural regions of the United States and of one of the richest coal fields of the state. The city is also rich in memories of Abraham Lincoln, who lived in Springfield and practiced law there.

The farmlands of southern Illinois produce large quantities of soybeans, corn, oats, and wheat. Livestock raising is a major activity, and the state is a major producer of hogs.

THE NORTH CENTRAL STATES

Michigan

Michigan, too, was first explored and settled by the French, who founded Sault Sainte Marie in 1668. The area long remained wilderness, however, populated largely by Indians and fur trappers. British control lasted until 1796, and Britain again contested U.S. control in the War of 1812. In fact, the last British outpost in the United States was the garrison at Drummond Island, which was not evacuated until 1828.

Michigan is truly a Lake State. It consists of two peninsulas joined by the Mackinac Bridge. The lower, or southern peninsula, is bounded on the west by Lake Michigan, on the east by Lake Huron, and on the southeast by Lake Erie. The upper peninsula is bounded by Lake Superior on the north and by Lake Michigan and Lake Huron on the south. With its many miles of lakeside shore, Michigan is a popular vacation world.

The opening of the Erie Canal in 1825 and the Sault Ste. Marie Canal in 1855 contributed to the development of the state's rich mineral resources, and today Michigan is one of the country's major industrial states. Flint; Lansing, the state capital; Muskegon; Pontiac; and Port Huron are all important manufacturing centers.

Detroit, Michigan's largest city, is the traditional capital of the U.S. auto industry. It is also a busy inland port and center of a diversified industrial complex. Nearby is Ann Arbor, center of the University of Michigan, one of the leading universities in the United States.

Wisconsin

In 1848, when it was admitted to the Union, Wisconsin was still largely a frontier state. But as settlers poured into the region, the frontier character was soon lost. At the turn of the century, many Scandinavians migrated to the area, which was not too dissimilar in climate from the lands they had left.

Wisconsin is famous as a dairy state, and it is one of the country's major producers of dairy products. But despite the prominent role that agriculture continues to play in the state's economy, manufacturing has grown in importance.

Milwaukee, the largest city in the state, produces much of the beer consumed in the United States. It is also a commercial and industrial center and an important grain market. Madison, capital of the state, is the home of the University of Wisconsin, one of the most highly regarded universities of the nation.

Because it was so strongly opposed to slavery, Wisconsin withdrew its support from the Democratic Party in the years immediately preceding the Civil War, and the Republican Party was born in the town of Ripon in 1854. Superior, on Lake Superior at the western terminus of the St. Lawrence Seaway, is a major shipping center.

Wisconsin has ample vacation and recreation facilities. The shores of the Great Lakes are popular in summer, and winter sports include skiing.

Minnesota

The United States acquired the western portion of Minnesota in 1803 as part of the Louisiana Purchase, and Minnesota became a state in 1858. But real growth did not begin until after the Civil War.

The Great Plains states, from Minnesota to Kansas, pioneered in mechanized farming of large tracts of land. As early as 1870 large portions of the Red River Valley of western Minnesota were planted with wheat. Some farmers prospered, but the majority were bankrupted by drought in the late 1880s. Today the state's agriculture is more diversified, with sweet corn, oats, dairy cattle, and poultry among its major products.

Minnesota is an important producer of iron ore, mined from rich deposits in the Mesabi Range in the northeast. The state's forests are also important economically.

The Twin Cities, Minneapolis and St. Paul, are major industrial and cultural centers of the western Great Lakes region. Minneapolis is heavily industrialized; St. Paul is the state capital. Music, theater, and sports are all well represented in the Twin Cities, and many national corporations have their headquarters there. The lakes, rapids, and forests of northern Minnesota are popular with vacationers.

North Dakota

North Dakota was one of the first regions west of the Mississippi to be explored, and one of the last to be settled. It became a state in 1889.

The state is still predominantly agricultural, and it is one of the least populated states. Spring wheat is the principal crop. Industry is devoted largely to processing the state's agricultural products. North Dakota has abundant fuel, however. Western North Dakota has deposits of lignite; oil was discovered in 1951; and the state's rivers produce hydroelectric power, as well as furnishing water for irrigation. Bismarck, the state capital, is a major distribution center.

South Dakota

The first permanent settlement in what is now South Dakota was established at Fort Pierre in 1817, but few settlers moved to the region until 1874, when gold was discovered in the Black Hills area in the western part of the state. Gold is still mined in South Dakota, and the state has deposits of silver and lignite.

The eastern part of the state contains the fertile lands of the James River Valley. It is a grain producing region, with wheat the most important crop. Cattle are also raised there.

Pierre, a small city that was once a fur trading post, is the state capital. Sioux Falls, the largest city of South Dakota, is a trucking center and a major livestock market. The state's rugged but scenic Badlands and the giant carvings on the side of Mount Rushmore make South Dakota popular with tourists.

Nebraska

Nebraska was part of the Louisiana Purchase of 1803, and in the mid-1800s settlers drove the Indians who inhabited the region — Pawnee, Cheyenne, and Sioux — from the land. Nebraska became a state in 1867.

The land is rich, and Nebraska is a major agricultural state. Extensive farming and cattle raising is accomplished without irrigation. Eastern Nebraska is largely planted in crops, corn and other grains, sugar beets, soybeans, and potatoes. The western part of the state is the realm of the cattle rancher.

Omaha, Nebraska's largest city, is an important meat-packing center. Grain is milled there, and dairy products are produced in large quantities. Omaha also has a major lead smelter. Lincoln, the state capital, lies in the center of a rich agricultural region and is an important insurance center.

129

Rich in oil, stone, and cement, Nebraska is also known for its scenic beauty, including the buttes of the western part of the state that posed problems for the pioneers heading westward in their covered wagons.

Iowa

Although Iowa was acquired by the United States as part of the Louisiana Purchase in 1803, the first permanent settlement was made in 1833 at Dubuque. Iowa was admitted to the Union in 1846.

Iowa lies in the heart of a great, fertile plain, and the state has a greater share of its land under cultivation than any other state of the union. It is a major producer not only of corn but of soybeans, cattle, and hogs as well. And Iowa is an important center of meat packing.

Des Moines, the state capital, is a manufacturing and commercial center. Many insurance companies have their headquarters there. Cedar Rapids, a prosperous manufacturing center, processes agricultural products and produces feed, farm machinery, and electronics goods. The banks of the Mississippi River, which forms the state's eastern boundary, are lined with parks.

Kansas

Lying at the geographical center of the conterminous United States (the old 48 states), Kansas was the crossroads of all the trails that led to the West. This vast expanse of plains was first visited by Europeans in the 1540s, when the Spanish explorer Francisco Vasquez de Coronado pushed northward from Mexico. In 1803 the area became part of the United States through the Louisiana Purchase. By the mid-1800s, Kansas had become a bloody battleground in the struggle between pro-slavery and anti-slavery forces. It was admitted to the Union in 1861 as a free state.

Among the first acts of the early settlers of Kansas was the building of schools, and a reputation for stern morality was fostered by the campaign against the evils of alcohol and for Prohibition waged by Carrie Nation, who came out of Kansas to achieve national fame.

The fertile plains of Kansas produce tremendous quantities of wheat and support large numbers of livestock. In recent years manufacturing has grown considerably, especially the production of aircraft, mobile homes, and petroleum products.

Wichita, the largest city in the state, has a number of large aircraft plants. Kansas City, a major manufacturing center, has meat-packing and auto-assembly plants, as well as grain mills. Topeka, the capital, is a rail center and a manufacturing city. It is also the home of the famous Menninger Clinic.

Missouri

Although Missouri, acquired as part of the Louisiana Purchase in 1803, was admitted to the Union in 1821 as a slave state, it did not secede from the Union at the time of the Civil War.

Missouri is a land of plains that rise to the rugged Ozark Mountains in the south. Covered with forests, pitted with caves, and with large and beautiful springs, the Ozarks are a popular recreation area for middle America. The state has valuable zinc, lead, and iron-ore deposits and is an important manufacturing state as well as a major producer of agricultural products. Large quantities of corn, cotton, soybeans, and fruit are marketed, and the state's industries produce beer, meat products, and flour.

St. Louis, an important industrial center, a short time ago seemed threatened by urban blight and congestion. Today it is the scene of vast urban renewal programs and industrial growth. Kansas City is a major rail center and a major manufacturing town. Independence was the starting point of the Santa Fe and Oregon trails. Today it is best known as the home of former President Harry Truman. Jefferson City in the center of the state is the capital. Missouri is second only to Michigan in automobile production and fourth in shoe manufacturing in the U.S.A.

NORTH CENTRAL STATES
Description of the following pictures

page 133   MICHIGAN

DETROIT CIVIC CENTER

Downtown Detroit has undergone major redevelopment. Along the river front is the $100-million Detroit Civic Center. It includes Cobo Hall, one of the largest exposition buildings ever built. Adjoining the hall is the convention center, which is directly on the river.

GREENFIELD VILLAGE

This inspiring Village vividly portrays three centuries of American life. It consists of a Village Green and nearly one hundred historic buildings, which Henry Ford brought from different parts of the U.S.A. Meticulously taken apart piece by piece, board by board, and reassembled in the Village, the buildings are closely associated with great inventive and creative Americans such as Abraham Lincoln, Noah Webster, Stephen Foster, Wilbur and Orville Wright, Thomas Edison and, of course, Henry Ford. Dotting the Village are many craft shops, still in perfect working condition, where trades are practiced as they were many years ago by blacksmiths, glass blowers, weavers and candle-makers. There is even a tintype photographer. Greenfield Village is one of the great historic showplaces

of America. The photograph shows the Village Green with Martha-Mary Chapel and Clinton Inn.

page 134   INDIANA

MONUMENT CIRCLE, INDIANAPOLIS, INDIANA

One of the most pleasant features of the heart of Indianapolis, capital of Indiana, is Monument Circle. The circle's towering Soldiers and Sailors Monument includes the beautiful fountain that appears in the photo.

INDIANAPOLIS SPEEDWAY

The great speedway complex of more than 400 acres, including an 18-hole golf course, was developed from an automobile proving ground built in 1909. The famous 500-mile race, which is held each year on Memorial Day, attracts thousands of visitors and draws the attention of many thousands more throughout the United States.

page 135   INDIANA

UNIVERSITY NOTRE DAME, SOUTH BEND, INDIANA

This view over one of the lakes of the campus of the University of Notre Dame shows, on the left, the top of the administration building,

(Continued on page 141)

DETROIT CIVIC CENTER

MICHIGAN

*GREENFIELD VILLAGE,
VILLAGE GREEN*

133

MONUMENT CIRCLE
INDIANAPOLIS

INDIANA

INDIANAPOLIS SPEEDWAY

UNIVERSITY OF NOTRE DAME
SOUTH BEND, INDIANA

OHIO STATE FAIR
COLUMBUS

OHIO

THE STATE CAPITOL, COLUMBUS

MUSEUM OF ART, CLEVELAND

*WASHINGTON-MORRIS-SALOMON
MONUMENT*

CHICAGO, ILLINOIS

DOWNTOWN CHICAGO

STOCKYARDS, OMAHA, NEBRASKA

GATEWAY ARCH
ST. LOUIS

MISSOURI

KANSAS CITY

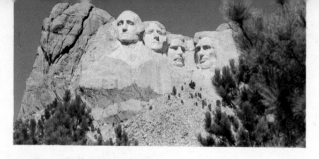

MOUNT RUSHMORE

THE DAKOTAS

BUFFALO

THE BADLANDS

THE LAKE WILDERNESS,
MINNESOTA

MADISON,
WISCONSIN

CHERRY HARVEST,
GREEN BAY

BRONCO RIDING, MUKWONAGO

WISCONSIN

FARMLAND

Description of the foregoing pictures
Continued from page 132

with its beautiful golden dome. To the right is
the magnificent tower of Sacred Heart
Church. Founded in 1842, the Roman
Catholic university has a campus of 1000
acres.

page 135   OHIO
THE STATE CAPITOL,
COLUMBUS, OHIO

*Ohio's capitol is an excellent example of
purest Doric style. Situated on a ten-acre plot
in the center of downtown Columbus, the
building was begun in 1839 and completed in
1861. In addition to state offices, it contains
a fine collection of historic documents and a
teenage hall of fame.*

OHIO STATE FAIR, COLUMBUS, OHIO

*Harness racing is popular in Ohio. In addition
to the races at the Ohio State Fair, one of the
biggest state fairs in the United States, there
is harness racing throughout the spring,
summer, and fall at about 90 county and
independent fairs in Ohio. The race at the
Delaware (Ohio) County Fair each fall is one
of the most popular.*

MUSEUM OF ART, CLEVELAND, OHIO

*One of the great collections of art in the
United States is housed in the Cleveland
Museum of Art. The attractive marble
building is situated in a beautiful park setting
in the city's University Circle area, a short
distance from downtown Cleveland.*

page 136   ILLINOIS
CHICAGO, ILLINOIS

*The second largest city in the United States,
Chicago is a key economic center of the
Midwest. A vibrant, bustling, ever-new city,
Chicago still contains monuments that recall
the past. The upper left photo shows one of
Chicago's many attractive monuments. It
depicts George Washington in the center
flanked by Robert Morris and Haym
Salomon, who played important roles in
helping to finance the American Revolution.
The lower photo shows downtown Chicago
along the Chicago River with the soaring
Equitable Building in the center.*

page 137   NEBRASKA
STOCKYARDS. OMAHA, NEBRASKA

*The world's largest livestock market, with the
largest stockyards, is in Omaha, Nebraska.*

141

The city is a meat-packing center, a distribution point for the West, a trading hub of the Great Plains, and a railroad center. Omaha is also a great grain market.

MISSOURI

GATEWAY ARCH, ST. LOUIS, MISSOURI

The 630-foot-high Gateway Arch is symbolic of St. Louis' position as the Gateway City to the West. A brilliant steel structure erected in the 1960s, the arch was designed by Eero Saarinen as a monument to the pioneers who settled the American West. In the background is the Mississippi River; to the left of the arch is the old St. Louis Basilica. Consecrated in 1834, it is one of the city's historic buildings. Its bells were made in 1772, and it contains paintings presented by the king of France.

KANSAS CITY, MISSOURI

A major center of manufacturing and trade, Kansas City lies in the extreme western part of Missouri, on the south bank of the Missouri River. The city's skyscrapers include the City Hall, which rises more than 400 feet. In the foreground of the photo is the Paseo Bridge, which spans the Missouri River.

page 138   DAKOTAS

MOUNT RUSHMORE

High in the Black Mountains of South Dakota, 25 miles southwest of Rapid City, sculptor Gutzon Borglum directed the carving of this tremendous monument in the solid granite face of Mount Rushmore, 400 feet above the valley. It shows in rich detail the faces of four great presidents of the United States — George Washington, Thomas Jefferson, Abraham Lincoln, and Theodore Roosevelt. Each face is from 60 to 70 feet in height. Mount Rushmore is now a national memorial.

BUFFALO

More than a third of the surviving buffalo of the United States are to be found in South Dakota. The greatest herd, with about 1500 buffalo, is found in Custer State Park, one of the largest state parks in the United States.

THE BADLANDS

In southwestern South Dakota and northeastern Nebraska lie the Badlands, a vast area with huge ravines, spectacular ridges, and some of the most unusual patterns of erosion to be found in the world. The region also contains many valuable fossils of prehistoric animals. A part of the Badlands has been made a national monument.

page 139   MINNESOTA

THE LAKE WILDERNESS, MINNESOTA

Minnesota, with more than 15,000 lakes, is a paradise for lovers of water sports. Opportunities for swimming, boating, and sailing abound, and there is excellent fishing. There is also fine hunting in Minnesota's fields and woodlands.

WISCONSIN

MADISON, WISCONSIN

Situated amid four lakes, Madison, the capital of Wisconsin, has attractive lake shore recreational areas. In the foreground is Lake Mendota and in the background, Lake Monona. Madison also has a beautiful capitol building, a famous university, and delightful parks.

page 140   WISCONSIN

BRONCO RIDING, MUKWONAGO, WISCONSIN

Bronco riding and rodeos, usually associated with the "cow country" of the southwestern United States, are extremely popular in America's dairyland, Wisconsin.

FARMLAND, WISCONSIN

Wisconsin, one of the leading agricultural states of the country, has more than 100,000 farms. Their rich green meadows are dotted with well-fed cattle. Wisconsin produces about half of the nation's cheese and a tremendous amount of milk and about a quarter of the country's butter. The state is also a major producer of vegetables, and it is famous for its fine fruit, especially cranberries and cherries.

THE WEST

COLORADO

NEW MEXICO

ARIZONA

UTAH

NEVADA

WYOMING

MONTANA

IDAHO

CALIFORNIA

OREGON

WASHINGTON STATE

ALASKA

HAWAII

THE WEST

Colorado, New Mexico, Arizona, Utah, Nevada, Wyoming, Montana, Idaho, California, Oregon, Washington, Alaska, Hawaii

The American West has captured the imaginations of men and women to an extent greater than that of any other part of the United States. It is a land of majestic mountains, forbidding deserts, and intimidating wilderness; but it is also a land of instant wealth — a land of gold, silver, oil, uranium. It is a land of ghost towns and vibrant, new cities; of the Grand Canyon and the Painted Desert; of warm Pacific beaches and northern forests.

The West is both the most mountainous and the most arid part of the United States. The Continental Divide, a ridge separating the watersheds of the continent, winds down through Montana, Wyoming, Colorado, and New Mexico. The precipitation falling to the east of the divide eventually runs off to the Atlantic Ocean; to the west of the divide, the waters find their way either to the Pacific or to the Great Salt Lake, in Utah. The region's mountains include the country's highest peaks — Mt. McKinley, in Alaska; Mt. Whitney, in California; Mt. Elbert, in Colorado; Mt. Rainier, in Washington; and Colorado's famous Pikes Peak.

The region is dominated by the Rockies, a vast system of mountain ranges and high plateaus that rise dramatically from the great plain that stretches westward from the Mississippi River. West and south of the Rockies are the deserts of Utah, eastern New Mexico, and western Arizona, creased by numerous mountain ranges — the Sacramento, Mogollon, Gila, Wasatch, and others. The great basin of Utah and Nevada is a vast, arid expanse stretching from the Wasatch range near Salt Lake City, in Utah, to the Sierra Nevada, in California.

The vegetation of the southern region of the mountain zone of the West begins with sparse, thorny, stunted scrubland, the home of the jackrabbit and the lizard. As the country rises to the north, the red hills and gullies are clothed with juniper, piñon pine, and small oak. The wet flood plains support cottonwood and clumps of mesquite. The southern mountains rise to a transitional zone of broad-leaved, deciduous trees; then come forests of ponderosa pine. At the higher altitudes of the south are spruce, fir, and aspen. The area is inhabited by a variety of animals ranging from the puma, a rather shy mountain lion, to the bats that are found in huge numbers in mountain caves. The most famous of the caves are to be found in New Mexico, in the Carlsbad Caverns National Park in the foothills of the Guadalupe Mountains. The Caverns, with beautiful stalactites and stalagmites, are mainly in three underground levels, the first 754 feet below the surface, the second 900 feet, the third 1320 feet. The southern mountains are also home to bear, elk, deer, and many colorful birds, including the mountain blue jay.

To the north, in the mountains of Colorado and Utah, a vivid world of mile-deep canyons, are stands of juniper, fir, spruce and pine. In that land where dinosaurs once roamed, today golden eagles soar and mountain sheep and goats leap over the rocks. Chipmunks are everywhere, and beavers dam the streams. The Rockies become lower in the northern mountain states of Montana and Wyoming. There, to the east of the mountains, are grain-covered prairies; to the west, deep, river-carved canyons such as Hells Canyon on the Snake River, which flows through Idaho to Oregon. It is beautiful country, with peaks such as those of the Tetons mirrored in blue lakes and with dense forests, the refuge of elk and bear and beaver.

Water has been the great issue dividing the states of the West. The Rio Grande and the Arkansas River rise in Colorado and New Mexico and flow to the Gulf of Mexico. But water supplies along those rivers often fail. The mighty Colorado, sculptor of canyons, and its tributaries drain portions of seven states as they flow from the Rockies through the Great American Desert to the Gulf of California. The waters of the Colorado have been dammed, ditched, channeled, and fought over for more than a century. The river has probably been the subject of more legislation and more litigation than any other waterway in the United States. The northern part of the region, however, is rich in water. The wide Missouri River has the largest watershed and is the longest of the rivers fed by the snows of the Rockies. The Snake, the Kootenai, and the Clark are rivers of Idaho and western Montana that carry great quantities of water westward to the Columbia and then on to the Pacific, where floods periodically threaten western Oregon and Washington. But suggestions that Columbia River waters be piped southward to water-short southern California provoke immediate opposition in the Pacific Northwest.

Although marked by an infinite diversity of climate and landscape, of economic activity and life style, the states of the West are linked by a dream, the dream of building a new life in a new world. The second half of the 1800s saw the beginning of a mass migration to the West, and the years after World War II saw another great movement westward. The Pacific was the goal of this more recent trek, especially California. And unlike earlier waves of migration, most of those involved were U.S.-born, not immigrants from foreign lands. Their goals, however, were not too dissimilar from those of their earlier, foreign-born fellow migrants — all sought a better life and more space in which to breathe.

Colorado

Colorado may be called the heart of the West, the embodiment of the free and open spirit associated with the pioneers who moved westward in the 1700s and 1800s.

Eastern Colorado was acquired by the United States in 1803 as part of the Louisiana Purchase. The rest of the state was acquired in 1848 from Mexico, and Colorado became a state in 1876.

Americans began exploring Colorado in the early 1800s, and in 1806 Zebulon Pike, exploring the Arkansas and Red rivers, discovered the peak now named in his honor. Others followed, including John C. Fremont, but the region remained largely the land of fur trappers until 1858, when gold was discovered near Pikes Peak. Mining has continued to play an important role as the state's silver, copper, zinc, molybdenum, oil, and natural gas deposits began to be exploited. Agriculture is dominated by cattle ranching.

A land of towering mountains, high plateaus, and plains, Colorado attracts many tourists. Mesa Verde National Park, in southwestern Colorado, is a favorite site. There prehistoric cliff dwellings indicate that the area was once inhabited by Indians who farmed the land. The fate of those early inhabitants is unknown, but severe drought some 500 or 600 years ago may have driven them from their homes. Aspen, once a silver-mining town, is now a popular resort for winter sports and the home of a summer arts festival. Colorado Springs is the site of the U.S. Air Force Academy.

Denver, the capital of Colorado, was once a brawling, gold-rush boom town. Today it is an elegant city with excellent music, fine museums, beautiful parks, and a truly cosmopolitan atmosphere.

New Mexico

New Mexico is a land of dramatic contrasts. More than 10,000 years ago there lived in New Mexico the oldest known inhabitants of North America — Sandia Man and Folsom Man; and in 1945 in New Mexico the first atomic explosion was set off.

The Spanish began to explore the area of New Mexico in the 1500s and made their first settlement before the end of the century. Santa Fe, the state capital, was founded in the early 1600s. The United States acquired the territory as a result of the Mexican War in 1848, and New Mexico became a state in 1912.

New Mexico is the country's major processor of uranium, and the state has deposits of oil, natural gas, copper, and potash. But there is relatively little manufacturing apart from the atomic energy industry. Cotton and grains are raised, as are both cattle and sheep.

New Mexico is a favorite with tourists, who are charmed by the Indian and Spanish elements that remain a part of the state's life. Pueblo Indians continue to live along the Rio Grande much as did their ancestors before the arrival of the Spanish. The Zuñi, famous for their silver and turquoise jewelry, have lived in pueblos south of Gallup since the 1600s.

Santa Fe is the oldest seat of government in the nation. Settled in 1609-1610, it was a Spanish colonial administrative center. Narrow old streets and Spanish colonial architecture give the city a distinctive charm. Nearby, to the northeast, is Taos with a stately Indian pueblo, an art center that combines the state's Indian and Spanish heritages delightfully. Albuquerque, New Mexico's largest city, was founded in the early 1700s. It is a combination of a sleepy old city and a lively new city, and it is a favorite health resort and tourist center. New Mexico's national forests and mountain resorts are also popular with vacationers and tourists.

Arizona

Arizona is a state of dramatic natural beauty, and its landscape is painted in bold, vivid colors. The Grand Canyon, the Painted Desert, and the Petrified Forest are all to be found there.

The Spanish began to explore the territory of present-day Arizona in the 1500s, and in the 1600s missions to the Indians were founded. The area became part of the United States in 1848 as a result of the Mexican War. Struggles with the Indians lasted until 1877, when the Apache were subjugated, and in 1912 Arizona was admitted to the Union.

Northern Arizona is covered by the Colorado Plateau. In the west is the mile-deep Grand Canyon. In 1919 a thousand-square-mile area was set aside as the Grand Canyon National Park. Grand Canyon National Monument, north of the canyon, was established in 1932. North-central Arizona contains the Painted Desert, a 200-mile-long region where erosion has worn away the surface cover exposing many colored rock surfaces. In the east is the Petrified Forest, which became a national monument in 1906. At one time it was a thriving coniferous forest, but its big trees were either blown down or fell down. Covered over by mud and silt for aeons, the trees eventually fossilized.

Southern Arizona is basin land crossed by mountains. Deserts lie to the west and south. Arizona's two major urban centers lie in the southern part of the state — Phoenix, the capital, and Tucson. One of the important cities of the southwestern United States, Phoenix is a lively combination of Spanish, Indian, and western American life. Roosevelt Dam on the Salt River provided water for irrigation that made the surrounding area an important agricultural region. Phoenix is also a center of industry. Tucson, with an Old World Spanish atmosphere, is surrounded by ranches and cotton fields.

Although now surpassed in importance by manufacturing and agriculture, mining continues to play a significant role in the state's economy. Arizona was once known as the Copper State, and copper mining and smelting continues.

Archaeological studies have shown that Indians lived in what is now Arizona for centuries before Europeans discovered the New World. Today the Indian population of Arizona is greater than that of any other state and some 30 percent of the state's area is occupied by Indian reservations. Flagstaff has long been a center for Indian festivals.

Utah

Utah, too, was explored by the Spanish in the 1500s, and the area was acquired from Mexico in 1848. The first permanent settlement had been made the year before, in 1847, when Brigham Young led a band of Mormons to the Great Salt Lake. The Mormons, members of the Church of Jesus Christ of Latter-day Saints, one of the major religious communities founded in the United States, had been driven westward by persecution. Established in New York State in 1820 by Joseph Smith, the Church of Jesus Christ of Latter-day Saints quickly won faithful adherents.

Under Young's leadership Salt Lake City was founded at the foot of the Wasatch Mountains in 1847 and the provisional state of Deseret was organized in 1849. The government of the United States refused to recognize the state, however, and in 1850 organized the Territory of Utah. Conflict between the federal government and the Mormon community culminated in what is called the Utah War of 1857-1858. Young stepped down as governor of the territory, although he retained his influence, and in 1896 Utah became a state. Today Mormons make up more than two thirds of Utah's population, and Salt Lake City is the headquarters of a world-wide community of more than 2 million Mormons.

Most of Utah lies on the Colorado Plateau, a vast upland region marked by canyons. The western part of the state is basin land. It includes the Great Salt Lake and the desert region. The Rockies dominate the center, where the Wasatch Mountains are found. Utah is rich in minerals, and there are valuable deposits of coal, copper, gold, iron ore, lead, oil, uranium, and zinc. Metal processing and the production of metal goods are important industries, and Utah is an aerospace center. Grains and sugar beets are important crops, and cattle is raised along with sheep and poultry.

Salt Lake City, the state capital, is visited by thousands of people each year. It is the center of the Mormon Church, and the magnificent Mormon Temple and Tabernacle are landmarks. The city is also a major commercial and industrial center.

Utah has many winter recreation areas, and there are fine camp sites in the state's many national forests and monuments. Among the most interesting of the national reservations is Dinosaur National Monument, in the northeastern part of the state, where large numbers of well-preserved skeletons of prehistoric animals have been found. Antelope Island, in the Great Salt Lake, is a refuge for the American Buffalo.

Nevada

Ever since the discovery in 1859 of the Comstock lode, one of the richest gold and silver deposits ever found in the United States, Nevada has been a mecca for adventurers.

John C. Frémont explored the region in 1843-1845, and the United States acquired the territory from Mexico in 1848. The first settlement was made in 1851 by Mormons, but few settlers were attracted to the land, most of which lies in the Great Basin, a huge barren area west of the Rockies. Population growth came with the discovery of gold and silver, and in 1864 Nevada became a state.

The fabulous Comstock lode, near Virginia City in the western part of the state, was played out by the mid-1880s, and today copper is the most important product of Nevada's mines. The state's most valuable source of income is tourism, and thousands upon thousands of people are drawn to Nevada's casinos, nightclubs, and posh hotels.

Las Vegas, originally settled by Mormons in the 1850s, was a struggling desert town until 1931, when the state legalized gambling. Today the city is a world entertainment and gambling center. Reno, once the haven of divorce seekers, is still in many ways one of the country's last frontier towns. Virginia City, where Mark Twain and Bret Harte once worked as reporters on the *Territorial Enterprise*, Nevada's first newspaper, still looks very much as it must have in the 1870s, when it was the mining metropolis of the West.

Nevada's appeal to tourists and vacationers is not limited to the gambling tables of Las Vegas, however. Carson City, the state capital, is a popular winter resort, and there is fine swimming, boating, and fishing at Pyramid Lake, Walker Lake, Lake Mead, and Lake Tahoe on the border of California.

Wyoming

A land of traders, trappers, cowboys, and lumberjacks, Wyoming is truly the American West. Overland migration through Wyoming over the Oregon Trail began in 1842, and the Union Pacific Railroad began to push through the territory in the 1860s. In 1890 Wyoming was admitted to the Union.

Wyoming's landscape is magnificent. Towering mountains dominate the northwest, where Yellowstone and Grand Teton National Parks are located. Yellowstone, established in 1872, was the first national park and it is still the best known; and Old Faithful may be the best-known geyser in the world. Devils Tower, in the northeast, established in 1906, was one of the first national monuments. Grand Teton National Park, to the south of Yellowstone, is spectacular.

All in all, some 15 percent of Wyoming's land is in national forests and grasslands. The state's forests provide valuable timber, and its prairies support large herds of cattle. Wyoming's rich mineral deposits include oil, natural gas, uranium, and iron ore.

Wyoming was a pioneer in extending full political rights to women. In 1868 woman's suffrage was enacted, a first in the United States. And Wyoming was the first state to have a woman governor, Mrs. Nellie Tayloe Ross, who served from 1925 to 1927.

Cheyenne, the state's capital, is a town of cattle and sheep ranchers. It is famous for its Frontier Days in July and August featuring rodeos and parades. Jackson, at the southern entrance to Grand Teton National Park, is a colorful year-round resort town. Casper is Wyoming's leading industrial center. Laramie is a trade center in a rich livestock-raising area. The University of Wyoming at Laramie has an excellent collection of materials relating to the history of the West and an outstanding geological museum.

Montana

The Lewis and Clark expedition explored the area of Montana soon after the United States acquired the territory in 1803 as part of the Louisiana Purchase. The discovery of gold in 1858 drew settlers, and conflict with the Indian inhabitants was bitter. In 1876 in the valley of the Little Big Horn, in southern Montana, a united force of Sioux and Cheyenne defeated George Custer. There are many other battlesites in the state. In 1889 Montana joined the Union.

One of the largest states in area, Montana is rich in natural beauty and in natural resources. Its mountains are popular with skiers, and the Going-to-the-Sun Road, which cuts through Glacier National Park in northwestern Montana and crosses the Continental Divide at Logan Pass, is one of the most spectacular scenic roadways of the world. The state has millions of acres of forests, and mineral resources include oil and natural gas along with copper, gold, lead, manganese, and silver. The state's industry is devoted largely to processing the forest, mineral, and agricultural products of Montana.

Montana is an important wheat producer, and the state's farms yield large quantities of hay, barley, and sugar beets. Livestock raising is the most important agricultural activity, and the state has large herds of both beef and dairy cattle and sheep.

The state's two major urban centers are Great Falls and Billings. Great Falls, on the Missouri River, is an important center for processing metals. Billings, in south-central Montana, is the center of the Midland Empire, an area rich in oil, sugar, and beef. Billings' fairs, rodeos, horse shows, and Western Week attract many visitors. Butte, high in the Rockies in southwestern Montana, is one of the world's great mining cities and has been called the richest hill on earth. Mines there have been worked continuously for more than a century.

Idaho

The Lewis and Clark expedition explored Idaho in 1805, and the Oregon Trail passed through the territory, which is marked by spectacular mountains and scenic lakes. The Snake River, with its awesome Hells Canyon, drains Idaho. Gold was discovered in 1860, and settlement followed. In 1890 Idaho was admitted to the Union.

Almost one third of the state is covered by valuable timber, and Idaho has many national forests. The soil is fertile and where irrigated produces large crops of potatoes, sugar beets, grains, and fruits. There is also considerable cattle and sheep ranching. Lead, phosphates, silver, and zinc are mined.

Although Idaho does not rank among the foremost tourist centers of the West, it does boast one of the most popular resorts of the region, Sun Valley. Year-round activities there include skiing, golf, water sports, hunting, hiking, and horseback riding. One of the most interesting of the state's natural features is to be found at the Craters of the Moon National Monument in south-central Idaho. There pitted landscapes with strange lava shapes from extinct volcanoes create an atmosphere reminiscent of a moonscape.

Boise, the capital and largest city of the state, was founded in 1863, the child of a gold rush. It is now a center for meat packing and dairy products. Coeur d'Alene is popular with water sports enthusiasts.

California

In 1769 Franciscan friars built the first of the chain of missions that formed the Spanish colony of California, and for decades after it was a quiet world of small Spanish pueblos. As time went on, settlers from the United States began to enter the region and, after brief skirmishes with Mexican authorities culminating in the Bear Flag Revolution, California was declared independent of Mexico in 1846. California remained independent for only a few days before becoming a part of the United States, and in 1850 it became a state.

Fringed by mountains along its 800 mile coast and bordered by another mountain system to the east, California has a wealth of natural beauty. Mountains and valleys, orange groves and vineyards, redwood stands and magnificent beaches fill the state. Sequoia National Park, with its giant trees, includes majestic Mt. Whitney, which rises to an elevation of 14,494 feet, the highest point in the United States outside of Alaska. Just some 80 miles to the south is Death Valley, 282 feet below sea level, the lowest point in the United States.

Equally sharp contrasts exist among California's population, the greatest of the 50 states. It includes energetic, ambitious, hard-driving men and women and drifters and dreamers and cultists; migrant Mexican laborers who toil in the fields and orchards and the campers, skiers, surfers, and sunbathers who lead a casual, relaxed life.

California is a rich state. Fertile valleys produce cotton, vegetables, and fruits; and there are rich deposits of oil and natural gas. Commercial fishing is excellent, and fish processing is a major industry. Manufacturing is widely diversified, but the state has long been a center of the aerospace industry. Although no longer the motion picture capital of the world, Hollywood is still a major center of the entertainment industry producing a large share of the country's television fare.

Gold fever gripped California in 1848, when the precious metal was discovered at Sutter's Mill in Sacramento, now the state capital, located in a region of fertile fields and orchards. To the southwest is San Francisco, rising on steep hills beside San Francisco Bay, one of the largest land-locked harbors of the world. Linking it to the Pacific is Golden Gate, a narrow strait spanned by the magnificent Golden Gate Bridge with a central span 4200 feet long. A major financial, industrial, and cultural center, San Francisco exerts a strong influence on the West. Nearby are two of the country's most prestigious educational centers, the Berkeley campus of the University of California and Stanford University. San Francisco has great music, opera, and theater, and it has become a mecca for jazz musicians. It is a cosmopolitan city, with a famous Chinatown and fine restaurants and shops that carry the world's goods.

Los Angeles, in southern California, is the state's largest city. It is a sprawling metropolis made up of many individual communities, each different from the other. It is a film and television center, and it has a major branch of the University of California, UCLA. Nearby are many large manufacturing establishments and many fine beaches — Malibu, Redondo Beach, Long Beach, to name but a few. At Anaheim, a few miles to the south, is Disneyland, the most popular tourist attraction in the world until Walt Disney World was created in Florida.

San Diego, a charming city near the border with Mexico, is both an economic center and a tourist center. It is a major port, with one of the world's finest harbors. Boat building and fishing and fish processing are major activities, and the city is part of the aerospace industrial complex. The San Diego Zoo is one of the most attractive in the United States.

(continued on page 183)

THE WEST
Descriptions of the following pictures

page 157   NEW MEXICO
INDIANS OF NEW MEXICO
Approximately 70,000 Indians live in New Mexico today, including about one-third of the 120,000 Navaho of the country. The men work as farmers and stockmen, the women weave rugs and blankets. Many live on reservations, and Window Rock, in the northwestern corner of New Mexico, is the center of Navaho government. The three photos at the bottom of the page were taken in Laguna Pueblo, west of Albuquerque. The town dates back to a small settlement founded in the mid-1400s. The impressive pueblo was begun in 1699 on orders of the Spanish governor, Pedro Rodriguez Cubero. The stone mission church was built in 1699. The feast of San José, or St. Joseph, patron of the pueblo, is celebrated on September 19, and Indians from all parts of the state visit the pueblo at that time.

page 158   ARIZONA
GIANT CACTUS IN ARIZONA DESERT
The giant cactus (also called Saguaro) is typical of Arizona's southwestern desert. Like a forest of trees, the cacti cover hills and mesas. There are unusually large concentrations around Tucson. The Saguaro National Monument in the Tanque Verde Mountains near Tucson is a preserve of 63,000 acres set aside to maintain Arizona's finest and most typical cactus plant. The picture was taken at Bartlett Lake, northeast of Phoenix, in Tonto National Forest. The average height of such a plant is thirty feet, with some reaching as high as fifty feet. The maximum age is about two hundred years. The fruit is eaten by the Indians.

MONUMENT VALLEY
Part of a Navaho reservation in northern Arizona and southern Utah, Monument Valley is famous for the red sandstone monoliths that rise hundreds of feet above the valley floor. A Navaho shepherd is driving his flock in front of the red pillars of Yei Brichei and the Totem Pole. The valley is rich in prehistoric Indian buildings and rock inscriptions.

page 159   ARIZONA
THE GRAND CANYON
The Grand Canyon of the Colorado River — more than 200 miles long, 5 to 8 miles wide, and more than a mile deep — is one of the most dramatic sights in the United States. The canyon, situated in northwestern Arizona, was cut by the Colorado River, which flows through it, and the geological history of the land is plainly revealed in the rock layers of the canyon walls.

(Continued on page 177)

NAVAHO MOTHER WITH CHILD

NAVAHO SALESMAN

FEAST OF SAN JOSE, LAGUNA PUEBLO

GIANT CACTUS IN ARIZONA DESERT

ARIZONA

→

GRAND CANYON

MONUMENT VALLEY

WEDDING CHAPEL

LAS VEGAS,
NEVADA

GAMBLING CASINO

FISHER TOWERS AND
LA SAL MOUNTAINS

UTAH

ZION NATIONAL PARK

THE MORMON TEMPLE AND WORLD ADMINISTRATION BUILDING,
SALT LAKE CITY

UTAH

OWACHOMO NATURAL BRIDGE,
NATURAL BRIDGES NATIONAL MOMUMENT,
UTAH

ASPEN

**WINTER
IN
COLORADO**

*VAIL ALPINE
VILLAGE*

164

GARDEN OF THE GODS,
COLORADO SPRINGS

COLORADO

CLIFF PALACE
MESA VERDE NATIONAL PARK

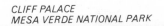

165

VIRGINIA CITY, MONTANA

WESTERN YOUTH, IDAHO

TWO MEDICINE LAKE, GLACIER NATIONAL PARK, MONTANA

HORSE RANCH, IDAHO

OLD FAITHFUL
GEYSER

YELLOWSTONE NATIONAL
PARK, WYOMING

FIREHOLE RIVER

LAGUNA BEACH

MISSION SANTA BARBARA

CALIFORNIA

YOSEMITE VALLEY

LOS ANGELES COUNTY MUSEUM OF ART

UNIVERSITY OF CALIFORNIA,
LOS ANGELES

MONTEREY PENINSULA

GOLDEN GATE BRIDGE, SAN FRANCISCO

CALIFORNIA

MOUNT SHASTA
(14,162 FT.)

170

LOST LAKE
AND MT. HOOD,
OREGON

RAIN FOREST
OLYMPIC PENINSULA
WASHINGTON STATE

SKYROCKET HILLS, GOLDENDALE

YAKIMA INDIANS

WASHINGTON STATE

MOUNT RAINIER (14,410 FT.)

HAWAIIAN GIRL

WAIKIKI, OAHU

HAWAII

IAO NEEDLE, MAUI

NORTH COAST, MOLOKAI

MT. McKINLEY (20,320 FT.)

ALASKA

ESKIMO CHILDREN
KOTZEBUE

ALASKA

OIL, DEEP UNDER ICE AND SNOW

MENDENHALL GLACIER

ALASKA RANGE

PETERSBURG HARBOR

Description of the foregoing pictures
Continued from page 156

page 160   NEVADA
LAS VEGAS
Best known of Nevada's tourist attractions is
Las Vegas, gambling capital of the United
States. The upper photo shows a street in
downtown Las Vegas lined with gambling
casinos advertised in brilliant neon lights.
Nevada is also a place where one can marry
quickly, and there are wedding chapels all over
Las Vegas. The city's 15 million visitors a year
have many luxurious hotels awaiting them.

page 161   UTAH
FISHER TOWERS AND
LA SAL MOUNTAINS
The snow-capped La Sal Mountains with Mt.
Peale (13,089 feet), the redstone Fisher Towers
and the green grounds of the valley combine
in this colorful photograph. In the foreground
flows the Colorado River, passing through
southeastern Utah coming from Colorado and
heading further south for Arizona and the
Grand Canyon.

ZION NATIONAL PARK, UTAH
Zion National Park, in southwestern Utah's
colorful canyon country, is one of the state's
great attractions. The Virgin River has carved
a gigantic gorge in the orange and red
sandstone, and tremendous stone masses stand

more than 8,000 feet above the canyon floor.
The national park, which covers more than
200 square miles, has excellent roads.

page 162   UTAH
SALT LAKE CITY, UTAH
The capital of Utah and world headquarters
of the Church of Latter-day Saints, Salt Lake
City was founded in 1847 by a group of
Mormons led by Brigham Young. The center
of the city is Temple Square, with the famous
Mormon Temple and Tabernacle and the
newly-completed Mormon World
Administration Building. The photo shows the
Temple, built of gray granite and with spires
more than 200 feet in height. The modern
skyscraper to the right is the World
Administration Building.

page 163   UTAH
OWACHOMO NATURAL BRIDGE,
NATURAL BRIDGES
NATIONAL MONUMENT
Utah is rich in unusual rock formations.
Natural Bridges National Monument, in
southeastern Utah, contains three natural
bridges. Owachomo, with a span of 180 feet,
is the smallest.

page 164   COLORADO
ASPEN
Once a prosperous mining town, Aspen today
is one of Colorado's best-known resorts. Its

←

GLACIER BAY, ALASKA

reputation as a winter sports center is international. Summer activities include lectures and forums conducted by eminent scholars and concerts and recitals.

VAIL ALPINE VILLAGE, COLORADO

On the slopes of Gore Range and Vail Mountain is one of Colorado's youngest resorts. Easily accessible from Denver, it lies in an area that was ranch country as recently as 1962. White River National Forest surrounds the resort.

page 165 COLORADO

THE GARDEN OF THE GODS, COLORADO SPRINGS

Northwest of Colorado Springs is one of the state's natural showplaces, the Garden of the Gods. Deep red rock formations are scattered over more than 300 acres of green grounds and small forests.

CLIFF PALACE, MESA VERDE NATIONAL PARK, COLORADO

Situated in southwestern Colorado, Mesa Verde National Park occupies almost 80 square miles and contains hundreds of cliff dwellings, pueblos, and pit dwellings. They were the homes of Indians who lived there from about the beginning of our era until the 1400s or 1500s. During the classic pueblo period, which lasted from about 1100 to 1300, highly developed habitations such as the Cliff Palace were created. Pottery of great artistry,

fine woven fabrics, and decorated walls have been found in the dwellings.

page 166 MONTANA

VIRGINIA CITY, MONTANA

Virginia City was born in 1863, when gold was discovered in nearby Alder Gulch and thousands of prospectors arrived within a few weeks. The city was the territorial capital from 1865 until 1875. Today the population is about 200. Many of the old buildings have been restored.

TWO MEDICINE LAKE, GLACIER NATIONAL PARK

Occupying some 1,500 square miles in northwestern Montana, Glacier National Park requires time to appreciate its unspoiled mountain scenes. The mountains are not the tallest, most have elevations between 8,000 and 9,000 feet, but the many glaciers are easily accessible and there are many beautiful lakes. The park extends on both sides of the Continental Divide, which is crossed by the Going-to-the-Sun Highway through Logan Pass.

WESTERN YOUTH, IDAHO

Big cowboy hats are popular all over the West and are worn by young and old. The corral of a horse ranch, shown on the next page, could be anywhere in the West.

178

page 167   WYOMING

YELLOWSTONE NATIONAL PARK

The first national park, established in 1872, Yellowstone covers an area of approximately 3500 square miles in northwestern Wyoming, southern Montana, and eastern Idaho. It is a wonderland, unique in the United States and in the world. There are spouting geysers, hissing springs, and boiling pools in all colors of the rainbow. There are mountain canyons and waterfalls with drops greater than Niagara's, and there are petrified waterfalls that constantly change their appearance. Most geysers are unpredictable, but Old Faithful, the most famous geyser, erupts at regular intervals of about 80 minutes.

page 168   CALIFORNIA

LAGUNA BEACH, CALIFORNIA

Multicolored flowers of breathtaking beauty frame the white sands that line the blue-green sea at Laguna Beach, a haven for artists in southern California.

MISSION SANTA BARBARA, CALIFORNIA

The Franciscan missions founded in the second half of the 1700s were the first European outposts in California. Father Junípero Serra founded the first mission, San Diego, in 1769, the beginning of the famous chain of missions that continued northward to San Francisco. Father Serra did not live to see

Santa Barbara established, however. The tenth mission in the chain, Santa Barbara was dedicated in 1786 by Father Lasuén. The mission has been in continuous use since its dedication.

YOSEMITE VALLEY, CALIFORNIA

Yosemite Valley is the center of Yosemite National Park, in central California. The park's lofty cliffs, high waterfalls, and stands of giant sequoias make it a popular site. To the left in the photo is El Capitan; far in the background is Half Dome and the abrupt prominence of Clouds Rest; to the right is Sentinel Dome and the Cathedral Rocks, which frame the romantic Bridalveil Fall, with a drop of more than 600 feet.

page 169   CALIFORNIA

LOS ANGELES COUNTY MUSEUM OF ART, CALIFORNIA

The attractive modern exterior of the Los Angeles County Museum of Art gives exciting promise of the treasures to be found inside. The museum consists of three buildings connected by covered walks. The buildings open on a large exhibition area for sculpture. The splendid permanent collections range from prehistoric art through 20th century works and include both Asian and Western arts.

UNIVERSITY OF CALIFORNIA, LOS ANGELES

UCLA, as the Los Angeles campus of the vast University of California is popularly known, ranks with the major universities of the world. Its architecture runs a colorful gamut from Italian Renaissance to stark modern.

MONTEREY PENINSULA, CALIFORNIA

With its varied shoreline of rocks, reefs, and sandy beaches, Monterey Peninsula has a unique charm. One of the great scenic experiences is the Seventeen-Mile Drive on Monterey Peninsula, which offers some of the most beautiful views of the California coast. The Drive starts at Pacific Grove and follows the coastline to Carmel. The photograph shows the rock at Midway Point, one of the highlights of this drive.

page 170   CALIFORNIA

GOLDEN GATE BRIDGE, SAN FRANCISCO, CALIFORNIA

Near and far shapes have a peculiar clarity in the fog that moves in through Golden Gate. Clear and brilliant in the distance is the skyline of San Francisco, the heart of northern California. Golden Gate Bridge connects northern California with the peninsula of San Francisco. Completed in 1937, the bridge rises 746 feet above the water with a central span of 4,200 feet in length and

the minor spans at either end each 1,125 feet in length.

MOUNT SHASTA (14,162 feet)

Like a gigantic white crystal, Mount Shasta stands out over northern California, visible from far away with its snow-covered peak and its monumental outline. Looking up from Strawberry Valley to the belt of dark conifers at the edge of snowfields, the photograph shows the southwestern slopes of Mount Shasta in a mild afternoon sun.

page 171

LOST LAKE AND MT. HOOD, OREGON

Snow-capped Mt. Hood, 11,235 feet high, rises in northwestern Oregon. It is the state's highest mountain. Its beauty is revealed in views such as this from Lost Lake, a popular vacation site. One of the extinct volcanoes of the Cascades, Mt. Hood is covered with glaciers that extend to the timber line.

RAIN FOREST, OLYMPIC PENINSULA, WASHINGTON

Rivers and valleys cut into the large Olympic Peninsula, with its little-explored wilderness area. The temperate rain forests of the peninsula contain trees hundreds of years old covered with lichen and moss. The vegetation is as lush as that of the tropics.

page 172 WASHINGTON STATE

SKYROCKET HILLS, GOLDENDALE
YAKIMA INDIANS

Southeastern Washington has vast wheat fields. The golden bounty of the rolling Skyrocket Hills colors the landscape around Goldendale. Washington has a considerable Indian population, and the photo shows a group of Yakima Indians in festive costumes on their way to a rodeo.

MT. RAINIER (14,410 feet)

Night is over the valley and the lights still burn in Yakima Park, but the first rays of the sun brighten the snow and the glacier-capped summit of Mt. Rainier, which rises to an elevation of 14,410 feet in the Cascades, in this view from the northeast. The peak, now part of a national park, is the highest mountain in the Cascades and in the state.

page 173 HAWAII

HAWAIIAN GIRL

The Hawaiians have been called the golden people. They combine the best of the East and the West, and the combination of Polynesian, Malay, Japanese, Chinese, and European heritage has produced a new type of human being — friendly, kind, hospitable. They welcome you to their islands with their traditional greeting, Aloha (welcome), with flowers, and perhaps, a kiss. Hawaiians are indeed a new human type.

WAIKIKI, OAHU

Palm-studded Duke Kahanamoku Beach is one of the most beautiful on Oahu. This is the western end of famous Waikiki Beach, on the southern coast of Oahu.

MOLOKAI

Molokai is one of the most beautiful but seldom visited of the Hawaiian Islands. Although there are good roads along the southern coast and through the western part of the island, no road leads through the wild north coast shown in this photo taken from an airplane. The steep, green-clad cliffs rise as high as 3000 feet, and waterfalls drop from many of them.

IAO NEEDLE, MAUI

A plant-covered rock formation, the Iao Needle rises 1200 feet above the narrow Iao Valley, and more than 2200 feet above sea level. A major battle was fought there in 1790 by Kamehameha the Great, who united the islands into a single kingdom, and Kalanikupule, king of Maui. It is said that so many Maui warriors were slain that their bodies dammed up the Iao River.

page 174 ALASKA

MT. McKINLEY

Mt. McKinley, rising more than 20,320 feet in south-central Alaska, is the nation's highest mountain. It is in the center of a

3000-square-mile national park. Covered with glaciers and snow, it is visible from great distances and gleams brilliantly on clear days. But often it is covered by clouds.

ESKIMO CHILDREN, KOTZEBUE, ALASKA

The Arctic region of Alaska is the home of the Eskimo. They live in small villages, with Barrow and Kotzebue their largest settlements. The Eskimo are very friendly, and the children find having their picture taken great fun.

page 175   ALASKA

OIL, DEEP UNDER THE ICE AND SNOW

One of the world's richest oil deposits was discovered in the barren North Slope area of Alaska's Arctic in the 1960s. Drilling and construction workers at camps such as this in the tundra north of the Brooks Range have comfortable quarters, even though outside temperatures drop to –60°F and below. A major problem is how to move the crude oil in Arctic cold, through fierce blizzards, over frozen, snow-covered terrain.

MENDENHALL GLACIER, ALASKA

Mendenhall Glacier is moving to the shore very close to Alaska's capital, Juneau. Just behind the city lie ice fields, the Juneau Ice Cap, which cover an area of more than 1200 square miles.

ALASKA RANGE

Like brilliant white crystals, the snow-capped mountains of the Alaska Range stand out from the green, swampy lowlands to the south. The Alaska Range runs in a half circle through the center of southwestern Alaska starting southwest of Cook Inlet, curving eastward at Mt. McKinley, and ending on the Yukon border.

PETERSBURG HARBOR, ALASKA

The colorful harbor of Petersburg, south of Juneau, is a center of salmon and shrimp fishing.

page 176   ALASKA

GLACIER BAY, ALASKA

From Tarr Inlet of Glacier Bay one has a clear view of towering Mt. Fairweather, which rises 15,300 feet, and, on the left, of Margerie Glacier streaming down Mt. Quincy Adams to the inlet. The area is part of Glacier Bay National Monument, in southern Alaska not far from Juneau, the state capital. The more than 2 million acres included in the monument contain 16 active tidewater glaciers. The waters of the bay are dotted with icebergs, cracked off from near-vertical ice cliffs. Glaciers, deep fiords, and snow-covered mountains combine with lush forests and abundant wildlife to create a unique wilderness.

(Continued from page 155)
Oregon

Oregon is as famous for its rugged, rocky coastline as for its great mountain ranges and vast stands of timber. U.S. claims to the territory date from 1792, when Capt. Robert Gray discovered the Columbia River. The Lewis and Clark expedition explored the area in 1804-1806, and in 1842 the first settlers arrived over the Oregon Trail. Oregon became a state in 1859.

A narrow coastal plain rises to the Coast Range, a fairly low ridge. Between the Coast Range and the Cascade Mountains, which run north-south and divide the state, lie fertile valleys. East of the Cascades are plains scored by deep gorges. The Snake River, which flows through a gigantic gorge, forms part of Oregon's eastern boundary. Part of the state's northern boundary is formed by the Columbia River, which has many beautiful waterfalls. The highest fall is Multanomah, with a drop of more than 500 feet. Crater Lake, renowned for its brilliant blue water, fills the crater of an extinct volcano in Crater Lake National Park in the Cascades.

Oregon is a prosperous state. Timber, salmon, and tourists are mainstays of the state's economy, and Oregon produces ships, electrical and electronic equipment, and processes metals, particularly aluminum. The fertile valleys produce wheat and fruits and support large herds of dairy cattle. Bonneville Dam on the Columbia River supplies ample electric power.

Portland, Oregon's principal city and a major west coast port, is set against a backdrop of snow-capped mountains. It lies astride the Willamette River, whose fertile valley yields fine crops of strawberries and beans. A major wheat shipper and wool center, Portland also has a major livestock market. Seaside, at the Pacific end of the Oregon Trail, is the state's largest and oldest ocean resort. Salem, the state's capital, is a fruit and vegetable processing center; and Eugene is an important lumbering center. Pendleton, headquarters of Umatilla National Forest, is known for its annual rodeo and Indian pageant.

Washington

The area of present-day Washington was visited by Spanish, Russian, British, and French explorers during the century and a half between the 1640s and the 1790s. The first European settlement was made by the Spanish in 1791, but it lasted only a few months. The Lewis and Clark expedition visited the region in 1805, and the first permanent settlement was made in 1845. Other major settlements followed in the 1850s, and in 1889 Washington became a state.

The state is divided into two main regions by the snow-clad Cascade Mountains. East of the Cascades are broad plains well-watered by the Columbia River. It is an area of fertile farms and extensive wheat fields. In the west the Cascades are paralleled by the low Coast Range. Between the two ranges is a land of rushing rivers, deep gorges, dense forests, and rich valleys.

Washington is an important industrial state, a center of the aerospace industry. Shipbuilding and the processing of forest and farm products are also significant activities. Tourism is important, and many people are attracted to the state by its mountains. Winter sports are popular, and there are many winter resorts.

Seattle, with a fine harbor on Puget Sound, was settled in 1851. It was a jumping-off point for the Alaska gold rush at the end of the 1800s, and today it is a major Pacific port. The largest city in the state, Seattle is a major center of industry. It is the site of the University of Washington. Nearby Tacoma, also on Puget Sound, was founded in 1852. It too is a busy port and industrial city, and it contains a major copper refinery. Olympia, the state capital, lies at the southern end of Puget Sound. It was founded in 1846. Spokane, in eastern Washington, is the state's second city. It is an important economic center of the great Inland Empire. Surrounding farmland produces large quantities of wheat and fruits, and there are many industries.

Alaska

Approximately a fourth of Alaska, the largest state in area and the smallest in population, lies north of the Arctic Circle. At the town of Barrow, the northernmost settlement of the United States, the sun does not set for more than 80 days in summer and it does not rise above the horizon for more than 50 days in winter.

The first Europeans to settle in Alaska were Russians, who began to build their first settlements at the end of the 1700s. The indigenous population consisted of Eskimo, Aleuts, and American Indians. The United States purchased Alaska from Russia in 1867, and for many years it was referred to as "Seward's Folly" for President Lincoln's secretary of state at the time, William Seward.

The vast territory was largely ignored until the discovery of gold in 1880. The rich Klondike strike in the Yukon in 1896 brought a mounting tide of prospectors. After the gold fever abated, Alaska was again largely ignored until World War II, when the Japanese occupied two of the westernmost islands of the Aleutians, in June 1941, and the U.S. Army began construction of the great Alaska Highway. A two-lane gravel road, the highway was opened to unrestricted travel in 1947, but motorists are faced by washouts in spring and early summer and dust clouds in fall. Alaska became the 49th state in 1959.

Alaska is rich in minerals and timber, and its waters are rich in fish. Great oil deposits were discovered in the 1960s, and U.S. military bases are an important source of income. Alaska has much to offer the tourist, although many of the state's attractions can be reached only by chartered airplane. Large and small glaciers may be seen at Glacier Bay National Monument, in southeastern Alaska, and the nation's highest mountain, Mt. McKinley, which rises 20,320 feet, is in Mt. McKinley National Park, in south-central Alaska.

Fairbanks, terminus of the Alaska Highway, is still the heart of Alaska's gold-mining industry. It is also the site of the University of Alaska. Anchorage, the state's largest city, is the site of U.S. Army and Air Force bases. Juneau, the state capital, was founded as a result of the first gold strikes in the early 1880s. It is a port city with major salmon-canning facilities. Behind the city, mountains rise to heights of 3000 feet. Sitka, the administrative center of Russian Alaska, was once a major Pacific-coast commercial center. Alaska's largest totem pole, *Fog Woman*, more than 50 feet tall, can be seen at Sitka.

Hawaii
The 50th state, Hawaii lies in the Pacific Ocean some 2000 miles west of the mainland. The state consists of some 20 islands, which Mark Twain described as the loveliest fleet of islands anchored in any ocean.

The first European to reach Hawaii was the English navigator Capt. James Cook, in 1778, who called them the Sandwich Islands. Hawaii was united in 1795 under a

Hawaiian king, Kamehameha, who ruled until 1819, and by the mid-1800s the island kingdom had won international recognition. Later rulers proved less able, and in 1893 the last Hawaiian monarch, Queen Liliuokalani, was deposed. A republic was proclaimed in 1894, and in 1898 the islands were annexed by the United States.

U.S. settlers had begun to acquire land in the islands in the 1800s, and some grew wealthy from sugar and pineapple plantations. Large numbers of Asians were brought to the islands to work the plantations, and today Hawaii's population includes large numbers of people of Japanese, Filipino, and Chinese origins. Intermarriage has been frequent, and today there are few unmixed descendents of the islands' original Hawaiian inhabitants.

Hawaii was the scene of the first great battle of World War II for the United States when the Japanese attacked the U.S. naval base at Pearl Harbor. The islands played an important role throughout the campaigns in the Pacific, and in 1959 Hawaii became a state.

The major islands of the state are Hawaii, Kauai, Lanai, Maui, Molokai, Niihau, and Oahu. Hawaii is the largest in area, Maui, is the second largest; Oahu is the most populous. Geologically, the islands are in the process of building, for they are the tops of a mountain chain forced upward from the ocean floor by volcanic activity. There is considerable volcanic activity, and in 1960, for example, 500 acres of new land came into being as a result of volcanic eruptions. Hawaii has two active volcanoes, Mauna Loa and Kilauea. Legend has it that Kilauea is the home of Pele, the fire goddess.

Honolulu, the state capital, lies on Oahu, one of the most densely populated areas of the world. Honolulu has undergone spectacular growth since 1930. Land values have soared as luxury high-rise hotels and apartments have gone up and up. Banking and commerce have also grown. Today Waikiki Beach, lined with hotels and apartment houses, is alive with tourists.

The island of Hawaii, with its tall peaks and active volcanoes, its forests and waterfalls, attracts many tourists. The island of Lanai is almost covered by pineapple fields.

Fish are plentiful in the waters around the islands, with tuna and bonito the major catches, and Humpback whales may be seen in the water.

Hawaii is more than pineapples and surfboards, the muumuu and the aloha shirt, however. Hawaii is the Pacific hub of the world-wide satellite communication system, COMSAT, and the island of Maui has a satellite and missile tracking station. One of the world's largest telescopes is on Mauna Kea. The University of Hawaii is a major educational center, and Hawaii is a center of oceanographic research. All are representative of the world of tomorrow, which the United States has symbolized for so long for so many people.

ENVOI

The United States of America . . . Sweet gum trees and scuppernong wine. Aspen leaves blown silver by the wind on the slopes of the Rockies. Hound dogs baying at raccoons in the moonlight. Clam-bakes on a Maine coast. Watching the northern lights from a car going across North Dakota. The click of roulette balls in Las Vegas. Cable cars clicking up the hills of San Francisco.

The United States . . . Spires above the mist in Manhattan, higher than the topless towers of Ilium. A big, black pianist belting out "Am I Blue" in New Orleans. Cape Cod, with its dunes, where men signed the Mayflower Pact before they landed on that stern and rockbound coast. The battlefield of Cold Harbor, Virginia, where Grant lost seven thousand men in a few hours of fighting.

Everybody knows it is the land of the free and the home of the brave. It has welcomed immigrants since Indians showed the Puritan settlers in Massachusetts how best to plant corn, and Pocahontas saved Captain John Smith's life in Virginia. It is still being kind to hundreds of thousands of Cubans who have come by small boat, raft and plane to Florida in recent years.

ENVOI

Whatever else it is, this nation has always been foot-loose. Locomotion has been a prime preoccupation of the population from the beginning. Among the results have been covered wagons, motorcycles, snow-mobiles, swamp buggies, airplanes, and air-boats, the clipper ships of New England and — yes — also automobiles.

The people of the United States have given the world the ten-gallon hat and Western movies, and all the scenery that goes with them. Names like Cripple Creek, Wounded Knee and Death Valley help tell the story of the lonely frontier outposts. The howl of coyotes on a mesa in Oklahoma is part of it.

The country has not only given the world cowboys and Indians, but also the first men to camp out on the moon. Cape Canaveral today looks very much as it did when the Spaniards sailed by in the sixteenth century and gave it its name, in reference to its cane-brakes. It is a frontier, where lonely rockets and a few massive buildings are the only structures on the horizon for miles, and visitors can often see the American eagles that nest there flying over the cane-brakes. They can also see alligators and armadillos, immigrants from Texas to Florida.

The marvelous thing about the United States is the fact that its people really can go from sea to shining sea, feeling all the way, "This is mine, my native land." All across the country they will find the kindness of strangers.

Somebody in Silverton, Colorado, will tell you just how to get to the ghost town, Las Animas. Somebody in Oregon will show you how to dig clams. If you get stuck with a blown out tire, somebody will stop to offer you his spare tire, and help you change it. If you cannot find a motel room late at night, the filling station attendant may invite you to his home. There is no country in the world where so much is donated for a good cause, no country where people are so full of good will toward a new neighbor, a stranger.

America is a sort of poetry, and its spirit, like poetry, "finds its way to something in man which is obscure and latent, something that is older than the present organization of his nature."

ACKNOWLEDGEMENT

In preparing a book about so vast a subject as the United States of America, it is impossible to know and to describe everything from one's own observation. I am indebted to the many writers who have described and discussed the United States and its cities, states, regions, and territories.

Jane Wood Reno assisted me in my work, and helped prepare the text for publication. On my many trips across the United States I had valuable assistance in many ways from agencies of state and local governments, from airlines, and from friends. They gave freely of information and also, at times, assisted with photographs. The beautiful winter pictures of Colorado, and one of Alaska, are by Bob Bishop. The magnificent photograph of Mt. McKinley came from Bob Spring, Alaska Airlines; the stockyards of Omaha, from the Nebraska Game and Parks Commission; the views of Ohio, from the Ohio Development Department.

My special thanks go to the Alabama Bureau of Information, Montgomery; Alaska Travel Division, Juneau; Alaska Airlines, Seattle; Arkansas Department of Parks and Tourism, Little Rock; Chicago Convention and Tourism Bureau; City of Detroit; Church of Jesus Christ of Latter-day Saints Information Service, Salt Lake City; Public Relations Department, Walt Disney World, Florida (all subjects shown in the photograph are copyrighted by Walt Disney Productions); Hawaiian Air Tour Service (HATS), Honolulu; Indiana Department of Commerce, Indianapolis; Kentucky Department of Public Information, Frankfort; Massachusetts Department of Commerce and Development, Boston; Minnesota Department of Economic Development, St. Paul; Convention and Tourist Council of Greater Kansas City, Missouri; Montana State Highway Commission, Helena; Nebraska Game and Parks Commission, Lincoln; New Mexico Department of Development, Santa Fe; New York Convention and Visitors Bureau and the Port Authority of New York and New Jersey, both in New York City; the New York State Department of Commerce, Albany; North Carolina Department of Conservation and Development, Raleigh; Ohio Development Department, Columbus; Oregon State Highway Division, Salem; William J. Riley, Mt. Mansfield Company, Inc., Stowe, Vermont; Capt. Howard Robinson, Gustavus, Alaska; South Dakota Department of Highways, Pierre; Tennessee Department of Conservation, Nashville; Texas Highway Department, Austin; United Airlines, Chicago; Utah Travel Council, Salt Lake City; Washington Department of Commerce and Economic Development, Seattle; Wisconsin Department of Natural Resources, Madison.

There are many more who assisted me, and my heartfelt appreciation goes to all of them.

— Hans Hannau

Books by **HANS W. HANNAU,**
each one containing a collection of magnificent color photographs and a dramatic
description by this well-known photographer and writer.

The large volumes:

THE CARIBBEAN ISLANDS IN FULL COLOR
with 86 color pictures

THE BAHAMA ISLANDS IN FULL COLOR
with 66 color pictures

BERMUDA IN FULL COLOR
with 86 color pictures

U.S.A. IN FULL COLOR
with 176 color pictures

IN THE CORAL REEFS OF THE CARIBBEAN, BAHAMAS, FLORIDA AND BERMUDA
with 96 color pictures

✱

The smaller popular editions:

ISLANDS OF THE CARIBBEAN
with 90 color pictures

THE BAHAMAS
with 68 color pictures

THE BERMUDA ISLES IN FULL COLOR
with 72 color pictures

THE NETHERLANDS ANTILLES
with 100 color pictures

BENEATH THE SEAS OF THE WEST INDIES
with 175 color pictures

TROPICAL FLOWERS
with 72 color pictures

✱

THE ARGO BOOKS
with 50 color pictures

THE CAYMAN ISLANDS • PUERTO RICO
ST. MAARTEN • ANTIGUA • CURAÇAO
ARUBA • ELEUTHERA